The Book of Ancient Wisdom

Lindon Brown

Copyright © 2019

All Rights Reserved

ISBN: 978-1-950088-89-8

Dedication

This book is dedicated to the people who have come to the realization that there is much more to life than what we are experiencing. The reverential fear of God will open the door to wisdom from the highest source in the universe, the almighty God. Get wisdom, understand deeper, and do not forget nor turn away from Him. Do not forsake him, and He will preserve you, too.

Love Him, and He will keep you. Remember, wisdom is the principle thing. Use wisdom and understanding; exalt her, and God will promote you, too. He will bring you honor because you embrace Him. He will place on your head an ornament of grace, a crown of glory, and He will deliver to you what you desire.

Acknowledgment

First and foremost, I must acknowledge the Holy Spirit of God that gave me the wisdom to write this book of proverbs in an easy-to-read format. I thank the support team from book writing Inc, Simon Walker, Jason Louis, Irene Pearson, and Austin Troy for all their help, and also my good friend pastor Toni Ogobegwu for all his support, his command over the English language with which he helped me, and his words of encouragement.

I would like to thank prophet George Bett who came to one of my conferences and told me that he sees me writing five books, which motivated me to start writing. This is my first book out of the five he predicted, and I am hopeful of keeping myself going. I also acknowledge the help I received from my daughter, Alisha Brown, when it comes to using the computer, pastor Peter Sam for his prophetic insight, and all my family and church members in London and over the world for all their prayers and support.

About the Author

I am Lindon Raphael Brown. I'm 64 years old, born in Jamaica 14th July 1955. I am the founder and director of Outreach International Healing Ministries (O.I.H.M). We have church branches in London, Ghana, and Uganda. I currently live in London, where I'm the Senior Pastor of one of the O.I.H.M churches, but frequently I travel to Africa, India, and Europe as well. I am also a conference speaker and a healing evangelist. I do missionary work and support an orphanage in Uganda. My vision is to help people in fulfilling their dreams and enabling them to become who they really want to be.

Contents

Dedication.. i
Acknowledgment ii
About the Author iii
Introduction 1

Chapter 1- The Beginning of Knowledge................................. 2
Chapter 2- The Value of Wisdom 8
Chapter 3- Guidance for the Young...15
Chapter 4- A Father's Instructions to His Children 22
Chapter 5- Avoid Seducing Women 29
Chapter 6- Financial Wisdom 36
Chapter 7- Keep God's Commandments and Live 44
Chapter 8- Listen to Wisdom...50
Chapter 9- Wisdom, not Foolishness 56
Chapter 10- Wise Instruction from Solomon...............................62
Chapter 11- Dishonesty Does Not Pay 67
Chapter 12- Whoever Loves Discipline Loves Knowledge 72
Chapter 13- A Wise Child Responds to His Father's Discipline.......77
Chapter 14- A Wise Woman Builds 82
Chapter 15- A Soft Answer Turns Away Wrath 88
Chapter 16- The Preparation of the Heart is Important 101
Chapter 17- Better is A Dry Morsel with Quietness, Than A House Full of Feasting with Strife...106
Chapter 18- For By Your Words You Will Be Justified, and By Your Words You Will Be Condemned..105
Chapter 19- Never Stop Listening..109
Chapter 20- Counsel in the Heart of a Person is Like Deep Water.114
Chapter 21- God Will Examine Your Heart.................................118
Chapter 22- Let the Words of the Wise Be Fixed Upon Your Lips..122
Chapter 23- Restrain Yourself from Too Much Wine and Food 126
Chapter 24- Don't envy evil men or desire to be with them, for their heart plan violence, and their words stir up trouble 130
Chapter 25- Wise sayings of Solomon 136

Chapter 26- Don't Respond To the Stupidity of a Fool.................140
Chapter 27- Never Boast About Tomorrow 144
Chapter 28- A Person of Understanding and Knowledge Right Will Be Prolonged..149
Chapter 29- Don't be blind to the wisdom of God......................156
Chapter 30- We need Yahweh 162
Chapter 31- The words of King Lemuel's Mother.......................168

Page Left Blank Intentionally

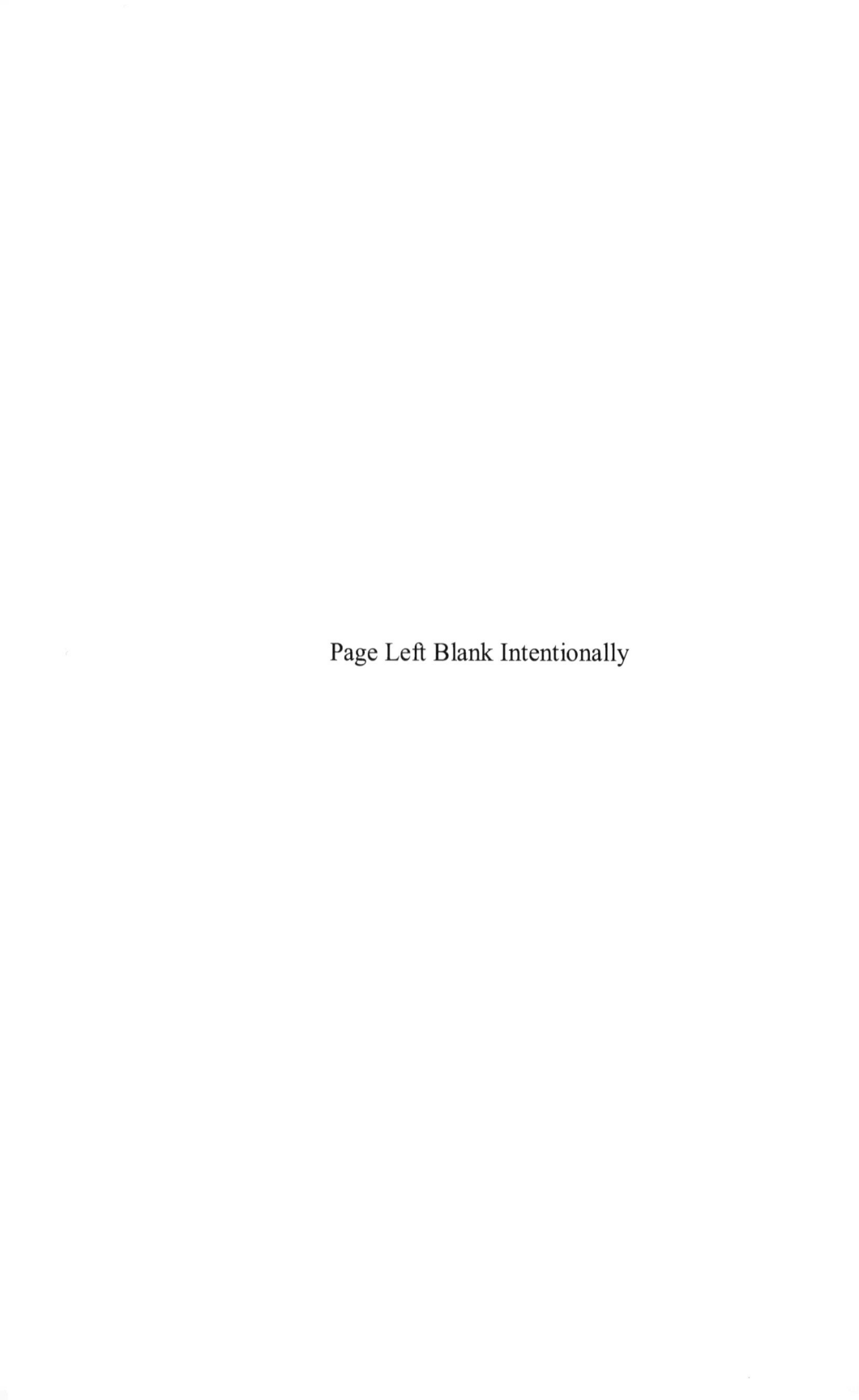

Introduction

Knowledge is the beginning of understanding humanity and the enlightenment of the soul. The source of the purest knowledge is the one true Being. This book explores the birth of knowledge from the womb of fear. It also finds the true meaning of faith and reveals how faith can bring wisdom, without which we are nothing but an empty shell.

In this book, we will look at the way of life our Lord ordered us to live. In His mercy, He showed us the way to prosperity and peace. The way to true peace and prosperity is by following the Lord's commandments. This book reveals how one can abstain from the way of evil and walk the path of true faith.

This book is a rewording of the book of proverbs in an easy to read format. There are thirty-one chapters contained in the book of proverbs. This book also explored the birth of knowledge from the womb of Reverential Fear, which leads us to the beginning of wisdom.

Chapter 1
The Beginning of Knowledge

What is knowledge? This is a question quite simple to answer in words, yet difficult to explain. Where did the knowledge come from? What gives birth to it? Where is that beautiful womb which nurtures the existence of everything? The answer to all these questions will come in a minute, but before this, let's examine what it is that we call knowledge. Right now, if you google the term *knowledge*, words like awareness, understanding, familiarity, fact, description, and many more will appear.

All these words will attempt to explain what knowledge is. But in its true and pure form, knowledge is none of these words, yet it is the reason for the existence of all these words. There are two types of knowledge. One is the knowledge that we gain about the world from textbooks. It is the knowledge about human life and is quite essential to have in order to survive in this jungle of humans. Without this knowledge, you are considered useless amongst your fellow beings. This situation is becoming true with passing time and technological development.

This knowledge has a distinctive quality, which makes its recipients proud of themselves. It makes its recipient fall into the delusion of being better than others and worth something. This is the type of knowledge that a man comes into contact with in his mortal existence. The second type of knowledge is hard to come by in this world of conspicuous consumption, materialism, and selfishness. This type of knowledge is the truest in its existence and form and takes precedence over any other kind of knowledge in this universe.

This knowledge cannot be learned, but it dawns on your soul and enlightens you, and brings you out of the darkness of ignorance. This form of knowledge is also very demanding. To find it, you need to lose everything. It demands submission; it demands you to be on your knees to raise you above your fellow beings; it demands your head bowed to give you the vision to see everything clearly. This type of knowledge comes out of the most unexpected place, and that is FEAR. Knowledge, in its true and purest form, takes its first breath in the soul of a human when they fear their Lord for the first time. How baffling is the statement that knowledge comes from fear! How can that be true? We all know what fear is; it is a crippling human emotion; it is the epitome of human weakness. Then how can something as profound as knowledge owe its existence to it? The answer to this question is that knowledge does not just come from any fear, but it comes from the fear of God. Only those who have a fear of the Lord in their heart can realize the limitations and weaknesses of their existence.

Those who fear God are bestowed upon with the ability to understand His words and the meaning and reasons behind His commandments. The wisdom then leads to the success of that person's mortal and eternal life. These are the people amongst us who are the owners of the wisdom bestowed on this earth upon humans. The Lord has promised them wisdom. He has promised them that He will make his words understandable for them.

The word of the Lord is the road to the truest form of all knowledge. Not everyone dares to bow or accept that they are nothing, that they still have a lot to learn. Some of us still believe that they know better. They believe that all they see is true, and anything that exists beyond the capability of human vision does not exist. They believe that everything happening around us is nothing but a cruel coincidence.

A coincidence that created life, and that now steers the course of our lives without the concept of divinity. These amongst us are fools, in actuality. The Lord has promised that one day they will know the truth. Then they will regret their choices. Then they will not think of themselves so wise. Ultimately, they will be on their knees and off their throne.

Then they will be the part of that dust from which they were created. At that time, even the benevolence of our Lord will not be there to help them. There is another kind amongst us. They are neither the wise nor the fools. They are the ones who heard the Lord's calling but refused to pay attention. They remain immersed in the wonders of their worldly existence.

They enjoy the temporary calm of their existence and forget everything. Then when the storm hits, they stand there without the shield of faith to protect themselves. They only turn back when the carefully woven web of their existence is disrupted by the cruelty of life. Then they turn and look for the one who has all the courage and all the answers.

The Lord in all His mercy then says to them, *"I am your lord, your creator, and the benevolent amongst all. I called you toward me in all my mercy, but you refused. You took the path that was smooth and shiny for a short walk. You saw the pebbles on my road, the slight darkness, and you left. You did not give me a chance. Now, why should I extend my hand to you? Why should I drag you out of the storm that you made yourself when the slightest struggle in my way was too much on you?"* The Lord laughs on their troubles and miseries and makes them an example for the believers.

The questions that we asked at the beginning of this chapter can now be answered. The first question was, 'What is knowledge?' The answer to this question is that knowledge is the realization of your weakness. It may be astonishing, yet it is the perfect answer. Once you realize that you are not the mighty creature that you believed you were, that is all it takes to gain the truest, purest, and the ultimate knowledge.

The second question was where knowledge comes from. Now you can comprehend that it comes from fear. The fear of our Lord gives us the knowledge of everything. It is the knowledge that everything that was created was created by our Lord. From something as marvelous as our universe to something as small as a plant growing on a sidewalk, all of these things are the creation of our one, true Lord. The next question was, what gives birth to it. Forgetting yourself gives birth to it. That is the most straightforward answer to this question. Another question that arises from this answer is that *how can you gain knowledge from forgetting yourself?* The answer to this question is that we are usually self-centered as humans. Everything that we see and experience from our eye, we experience it like us.

We never try to leave the shell of 'I.' Therefore, when we step out of the cocoon of our own existence and try to see the world for the first time, we see our Lord in everything. We see our Lord in our own physical human form. We see Him in the people we love. We see Him in the stone we step on, and the water that keeps us alive.

The last question was, where is the beautiful womb that nurtures the existence of everything or this knowledge. We are born with the answer to this question; all we have to do is close our eyes and see it within our souls. We will find a solution. In case you cannot figure out the answer yourself, here it is. The womb that nurtures knowledge is everything that our benevolent Lord has created. You are a part of that womb yourself that nurtures the purest and truest of knowledge.

Chapter 2
The Value of Wisdom

We learned earlier that divine knowledge stems from fear. Now we need to learn yet another aspect without which life is a barren desert, devoid of all good. That aspect is wisdom, which is a necessary ingredient for leading a life that is spiritual and suffused with the enlightenment of God. From the Philosopher's Stone to the Higgs Boson, if there is one thing that men of distinction throughout the ages have sought, it is wisdom.

The Lord has instructed mankind about the true worth and value of wisdom, as well as the fact that it remains immeasurable by earthly standards. At this point, you might be inclined to ask a question: *"What is wisdom?"* Though the word is brandished about, few people truly understand the essential concept of wisdom, the complexity of which would envelop the widths and depths of the ocean. Of those that do understand it, only a fraction would apply what their wisdom dictates them to do in their lives. Simply put, wisdom is listening to what the Lord says. And the Lord asks to keep on the straight path of righteousness and not stray from it, even though you will always be tempted to chase things that will only ruin you in the end. Those who are truly wise know what will benefit them in this life and the next. They know enough not to answer the temptations of everything that steal them away from the true purpose of their existence. They know not to be lured in by that which appeals to the eye, but only promises destruction beneath its glittery surface. Doomed are those who lose themselves and stray from the path of righteousness to the path of wrongdoing. And what is the one thing that will act as a beacon of light and keep you on the straight path? It is, without a doubt, wisdom.

Wisdom, like knowledge, finds its source in fear of God. However, wisdom is also something that teaches you the fear of God. In that sense, wisdom is quite paradoxical. Seeking it should be a part of your life's journey. Indeed, you must seek out wisdom as if it were silver because it is truly that valuable. In fact, the value of wisdom is comparable if not exceeding all the worldly treasures we label as priceless. No cost is too high to pay in exchange for wisdom. No risks and difficulties, even though they could be complicated and as high as the summits of mountains, are too significant in the pursuit of wisdom. For this reason, it must be sought with the same eagerness with which you would seek hidden treasures. When traversing the path of acquiring wisdom, you will discover the fear, as well as the love of God. Wisdom comes from God, as does knowledge and understanding. So, to increase wisdom, you must travel toward the Lord, as He is the source of all light and learning.

The Lord will tell you that to gain wisdom, you must first pay attention and then ask from Him. In fact, the path to wisdom begins when you turn your face toward the Lord and ask your needs from Him. It is this action that embodies your knowledge that only the Lord can cure you of your ills. So, you must raise your voice to the heavens and pour in your heart to ask it of the Lord.

Only when you do that, you will begin to find wisdom. The Lord will give you wisdom because from Him emanates all knowledge and understanding. It is only the fools who scorn wisdom, and they are the ones who are chiefly doomed to suffer from destruction. Forsaking truth and knowledge in pursuit of vain things will never yield fruits – in this life or the next. It is also a fact that one cannot be led astray unless one consents to it. So be vigilant and follow the path of virtue, for that is what leads to wisdom and eternal joy under all conditions. Now, you might ask: *"What constitutes wisdom? What are the things that the wise do, and conversely, don't do?"* To put it simply, things as knowledge, equity, and righteousness are the products of wisdom. Those who are wise of mind and heart find it easy to practice these qualities that are becoming ever scarcer in today's world. To such people, knowledge is welcome in all its forms. In due course, wisdom is what will keep them and liberate them from the ways of evil.

Therefore, make all your efforts to grow wiser – be wiser tomorrow than you were today. Gaining wisdom also means to incessantly find your way toward a hopeful future, even in a hopeless world. In short, wisdom does not just leave you with knowledge and understanding, but it also bestows hope and happiness upon you – all of which are vital elements to living an auspicious life.

On the other side of this equation are the people who abandon the path of wisdom. They are the people who are unfaithful to the Lord and to their true nature, with which the Lord sent them into this world. Such are the people who indulge in wrongdoings and sins. They don't wait for God's doors of mercy to open, and then, without even being aware of it, they end up injuring themselves. These are the people whose purpose in life is not to be wise. Instead, their mission is to be merely disobedient. In doing so, they end up where no man or woman wants to be. They land themselves on crooked paths that lead them in blind circles and never take them to the ultimate destination of mankind, which is exclusive to reach the Lord.

People who stray from the path of righteousness are soon trapped inside tunnels of darkness. No light awaits them at the end of these black pathways. In the world, such people delight in doing evil deeds. They find sheer pleasure and joy in following the ways of the wicked. In following along the road marked at every turn by transgressions, they soon fall into devious designs.

They seek their happiness, not in the Lord, but in going against Him. These are the people who are ensnared by the wiles of the seductress, who uses honeyed words to flatter them, so they are led away from the light. This is the immoral woman who has forsaken the companion of her youth and has forgotten her covenant with God. When a fool falls into her trap, he is unable to find his way back and is doomed.

So, pursue wisdom as though your life depended on it. In time, you will learn that wisdom is your guard and your protection against these transgressions. You will discover that wisdom is what beautifies your existence, and that it is what brings you the elusive honor that many runs after so relentlessly but are never able to find. Remember, wisdom, first and foremost, means seeking refuge in the Lord. You will only seek refuge in Him when you fear Him – when you fear incurring his displeasure and inviting his wrath upon yourself. You must always trust in the Lord for His way is the only way toward goodness and righteousness. He is the beginning of knowledge, and He is the eternal source from which issues forth the spring of wisdom.

It is only the upright who will find a place in Lord's Heaven. These, undoubtedly, are the people who put themselves on the mission of acquiring wisdom. These are the people who are just and righteous and owing to that, blameless. We all must do as much as we can to adhere to the path of truth, for if we do not, we will be amongst those who have erred and have only harmed themselves as a result. Who wants to be one of those who find no refuge in the mercy of the Lord, which is wider than the distance between the earth and the skies? Who wants to be abandoned and cut off from the earth? It is only the wicked who do that – through willfulness and choice. We all know where the various paths that we take in life lead. And we all understand where to procure the knowledge that would saturate our hearts and minds with the word of God. So, we must humbly hear what the Lord says to us.

Then, we must ask of the Lord what we need for; surely, He would give that which we seek and ask of Him. Prize wisdom, for it is far more desirable and valuable than the 'riches' that the unwise run after. This is the only true way to save ourselves from misery and ignorant death. The only way to lead a life of everlasting joy and happiness.

Chapter 3
Guidance for the Young

There will be times in your life where you will be lost. You will desperately need guidance. You will look here and there to find this direction which is missing from your life. However, the truth is that you do not need to look that far – you need to only look toward the Lord, for He is ever-present to show you the right way. The guidance comes from the Lord, who never falters to furnish you with knowledge and wisdom if you seek it earnestly. However, before the Lord gives you a clear direction, you must open yourself up to everything that the Lord has taught you through His Word.

The Lord asks of us not to forget and abandon the laws and limits that He has set for us. It is incumbent upon all of us who seek the Lord to preserve the commands He has given to us in our hearts. When we do that, we can follow the path that He has set for us successfully. This is our duty, and we must adhere to it with undying dedication and constant commitment. That, without a doubt, is the only way to find happiness and satisfaction.

Remember what the laws of God entail, and that we are wholly answerable to Him. This also means that we admit our dependence upon Him for everything. We must live by the guidelines He has ordained and be obedient to His Word. Thus, learning what the Lord has said and remembering it are vital elements to apply to our lives. We must bend ourselves humbly to what the Lord has willed for us; it is in this that we will find our deliverance.

We must remember that mercy and truth are with God. It is only our one true Lord who can liberate us from the tyranny of ourselves. Thus, submitting ourselves to the will and the Word of the Lord means finding our way to His mercy. It means gaining His regard and approval by placing our trust in Him. The Lord will guide us down the straight path by bestowing vast knowledge and wisdom upon us.

He is the only one who can because to Him belongs all knowledge, and to Him belongs all wisdom. We must then admit the greatness of our Lord, for He is worthy of eternal praise. Earlier, we learned about wisdom. You know now that God is the true source of wisdom. Thus, it would do you well that you acknowledge Lord's superiority over everything else too. Although we seek wisdom, that is only part of our purpose on this earth. We must never trust blindly in our understanding of things. This is because it is only the Lord who truly knows what lies behind facades. Thus, what we must do is put our trust in the Lord and ask Him to show us the way. We must always harbor in our hearts the fear of our Lord and keep away from all wrongdoings. This fear is a healthy one, for it will nourish our souls and sustain them in difficult times.

We must also not shrink back from dedicating all that we have in the way of our Lord. After all, what is the worth of worldly riches when compared to Lord's favors, which are everlasting? We must serve our Lord with what we have in our possession – if we use our material blessings to serve the Lord, then that is undoubtedly the best use of them that we could ever find.

Though the wealth and riches of this world are but transitory and inferior, they can't be used by us to earn our redemption profitably with the Lord. In this way, even those worldly assets that are insignificant in and of their own will become meaningful and significant. All of this is only possible if we pledge ourselves and our material belongings, the best of them, not to gain what we can from this temporary world, but to honor the Lord and His glory. What happens is that we turn away from the Lord at the first sign of affliction that we might encounter. Suffering in the world makes us question and go off in the wrong direction. We go into denial regarding the blessings that the Lord has conferred upon us, even during our toughest time, and we resort to anger and disobedience, for we feel wronged at being dealt with what we think is a lousy hand. However, that is not the truth.

The fact is that God sends difficulties our way only to discipline us. Trials and tribulations are a part of life. They are also necessary reminders for us to examine ourselves, identify where we have gone wrong, and find our way back to Him if we have gone amiss. We must understand that our Lord corrects us when we are wrong, and we must submit to Him to guide ourselves. Our Lord sends an infinite amount of good our way. He means only the best for us.

The Lord also asks us, as we discussed earlier, to seek wisdom. To increase in wisdom and gain more and more knowledge represent the ideal way to become truly rich. There is nothing at all in the world that can rival the benefits of wisdom; there is nothing that will bring as much contentedness and honor to our lives as wisdom does. So, when the Lord asks us to hold steadfast onto this path and work at acquiring wisdom, He intends for us to find all these things that are treasures in the truest sense of the word. What people do not realize is the fact that wisdom comes from the Lord; He created the world and everything in the skies and the heavens with His infinite wisdom. Thus, wisdom is an enviable quality to have because of its divine characteristics.

People who have learned the secret of the power of wisdom discover, much to their benefit, that wisdom serves them in all the ways that they could never have imagined. These are the people who have put their trust in the Lord – and because they have done that, they are fearless. They have nothing to fear because they have been given the strongest assurances by the Lord Himself, who is the Ultimate Guarantor.

The Lord has also asked us to hold on to wisdom. You might ask, *"How can this be done?"* Well, the simplest answer is that you can retain wisdom by always remembering the laws of the Lord – as we talked about at the beginning of this chapter. We must, first of all, acquaint ourselves with the things that our Lord has asked of us. Then, we must keep those teachings in our hearts and follow them with devotion, for that is how we will receive God's protection and the satisfaction that springs from it. If there is one guaranteed, fail-safe security lock against falling into evil and crooked clutches, it is to follow the Word of the Lord to its fullest. And only he or she who has wisdom can follow God's Word and abide by His Law. Although many dangers and fears will rear their heads in our lives, if we have received God's protection by living by His simple rules, we will remain protected from all evil.

We need not even worry ourselves about it for the Lord will save us from falling victim to all the instruments of evil. It is also true that we must never grow envious of what those close to us have been blessed with. The Lord has asked us not to deny the good that we may share with others and the good that others are worthy of receiving from us.

This applies especially to the people around us, the ones we live in close vicinity with. We must not harm our neighbors, nor should we imperil them in any way. What we must do is live peacefully with them. Furthermore, even though we may feel compelled to compare the state of sinners who have a lot of worldly gains, we must stop ourselves from following in their footsteps. Instead of looking to them for guidance, we must look toward those who have been redeemed by the Grace of the Lord. Such are the people who are good examples worthy of emulation. It is through such people that our Lord shows us the way and gives us the guidance that we seek in life.

Chapter 4
A Father's Instructions to His Children

Our Lord is always by our side, quite like a concerned father. He invites us to receive the guidance that we might be missing from our lives. He calls out to us and wants us to find our way back to Him. It is true that in life, a lot of us end up losing our way, for we are distracted by things that do us no good. The truth is that we need to be taught spiritual knowledge so we can serve our Lord diligently.

Our Lord wants to impart to us His divine knowledge and wisdom. But the question is, do we want to learn? Do we want to receive the instructions and teachings that only our Lord can teach us? As discussed earlier, knowledge and wisdom can be learned and received through impartation, but we must actively seek these virtues.

We must spend our time, as well as our worldly possessions, in the way of our Lord. This is how He will grant us His favor, which is immense and eternal. We must concentrate on this task, which is more pressing than we realize, so we can better understand the word of our Lord and abide in our life by it. God wants us to remember the knowledge that He has imparted to us. He wants us to keep His instructions alive in our beings, not just by memorizing them by heart but by applying them to our lives. To turn away from what the Lord has said to us means doing harm unto ourselves. During our mortal lives, we must make sure never to become distracted to the extent that we forget the Lord.

We must make sure that we do not end up turning our back to what the Lord has taught us. At this point, you might ask, *"What is that one thing that will keep us tethered to the word of God?"* The answer, yet again, is wisdom. As you have read here before, wisdom is what will keep you on the straight path and bring you back to your feet should you fall down on your knees through your human weaknesses or vices.

The answer is not to just gain wisdom, but to hold on to it. Remember, there will always be temptations and diversions that will take us away from the right path. Furthermore, there will be things that we will encounter in life that will seriously challenge our wisdom and might even try to divest us of it. We know that wisdom is a Godly quality. It is also true that wisdom comes only to those who seek it keenly and are willing to sacrifice for it. Indeed, it only comes to those who are obedient to the word of our Lord and dedicate themselves to living out a life that carefully follows the instructions that the Lord has already determined for us. As such, wisdom is a quality that has more merits than one can possibly enumerate.

We must also realize and acknowledge the real value and worth of wisdom, for it is the most crucial attribute to have in the world. It will not be wrong to say that for wisdom, no exchange of worldly possessions will be too expensive. Your wisdom dictates the means to follow the path of honor and virtue.

It means finding a way to redemption and deliverance. Our Lord has taught us wisdom. He has shown us the straight path – the one that will take us where His bounty lies. Therefore, by following along the path that the Lord has selected for us, we will never meet any obstacles that we cannot defeat using our human efforts. There will be no deterrents that will be too big for us to transcend, and there will be no difficulties too tricky for us to prevail over. Our Lord will ensure that we remain standing and that we do not stagger and fall onto our faces. He will protect us by bestowing upon us His Divine Grace. The only condition to enjoy Lord's Grace is to hold fast onto the instructions that He has given to us. It means never to let go of the teachings of the Lord and never forget what He has asked of us. Again, we must retain wisdom, for that is what will be our rescuer from a life of ruin and destruction.

Following a path of righteousness means our steps will not be hindered, and we will be able to make our way to our final destination without being waylaid by the distractions and temptations of this world. The Lord has warned us against those who neglect from the straight path. He has told us what they come to after having lived a life that led to their own irrevocable decline.

These are the people who find peace not in doing well, but in doing wrong. These are the people who embrace evilness and wickedness, as though those were the desirable things in life. These are the people who have turned willfully blind to the truth and have, by choice, forsaken the pathway to fulfillment. And what results come out of their defiance? Although they indulge in all sorts of hedonistic experiences that bring pleasure to them, all that remains for them is temporary and insignificant. The leisure they enjoy comes from harming themselves and others, and even then, it remains momentarily while their torment, which is a consequence of their wrongdoing, lasts eternally. The Lord has directed us not to follow in the footsteps of such people, for they are the ones who, in the end, incur losses heavier than they can manage. The wine of violence that they partake of so easily and so fearlessly comes back to haunt them eventually.

Then, they must answer for everything they have done while living a life of reckless abandon. They will have to account for an existence where they did not care at all about the word of God and where they chose to forget everything that He instructed. We must retrace our steps; in case we have fallen into the trap of what appears glamorous to our eyes from afar.

We must decide never to make such individuals our role models, for they will only take us to the ruinous end that they are carving out for themselves every day they live away from the wisdom of God. Avoiding such influences and preserving ourselves from the way that they might wield over us, in one form or another, is a requirement for living a life that pleases our Lord. Then, there are people who are just and equitable. These people, by virtue of their wisdom, which only propels them to do well, are as bright and illuminating as the shining sun. While others in their willful defiance show the way of darkness, these people show us the way of light. The Lord has told us to hold fast onto such people when we find them in our lives. Like lighthouses that guide stranded ships to the shores, such people are beacons of light that will, by their shining presence, steer you toward our Lord.

So, while the errant people will stumble and fall along the path of life, the guided ones will be able to move forward in a righteous way without any mishaps. We will only be able to follow the right path and keep away from the wrong one by looking in the right direction. This means shunning those who attempt, through various machinations, to lead us away from that which will truly make our lives worthy.

Our Lord shows us the way. He tells us where and how to seek wisdom. He tells us to keep a firm hold on our wisdom, for it is an irreplaceable virtue. To turn our face toward our Lord means to faithfully and loyally put our trust in our Lord's infinite wisdom. It means to submit ourselves to all that He asks of us, without doubts and without questions, for that is the only way of displaying our faith in Him. Transformation is a consequence of wisdom, and wisdom comes forth from fear of our Lord. Thus, we all must strive to remain steadfast.

We must pursue the path that the Lord, in His infinite wisdom, has decreed as fruitful. In short, that is the path we must follow without fail, for it is the one way to ensure that all we do in this life goes not in vain but is directed to serve the Lord and His Glory.

Chapter 5
Avoid Seducing Women

One of the things that the Lord in His infinite wisdom has taught us is to keep away from the sins of the flesh. In fact, the Lord strongly warns against sexual sins, which are an absolute recipe for self-destruction. Several times in life, you might be faced with temptations that invite you to fall into this grievous sin. If you listen to this voice of inviting sin, you will surely do harm unto yourself. Those who have a love of their Lord in their hearts are such people who can stand up and refuse the calls to go against God and the laws that He has set down for humanity.

Seducing women is an act that must be avoided at all costs, for it will lead to the destruction of your life; moreover, it will tear apart your family, the one you build with so much love and hope. It will bring dishonor and punishment on you and will leave you in a place of darkness. Wisdom tells you to run away in the opposite direction if faced with the prospect of committing this sin. Wisdom is to seek refuge if you are enticed and are at risk of committing this transgression.

Why do people fall into this sin of seducing women? There can be many reasons, but the root cause is the isolation from the wisdom that our Lord has sent to us. Then, a distanced relationship with your lawful spouse can be one of the reasons that might lead you to find fulfillment through this immoral act. However, remember that the Lord has instructed mankind to seek gratification within the covenant that is marriage.

If you allow your mind to move beyond the confines put in place by God, this only means you are willingly discarding the wisdom that He has taught to you. Can you claim not to know the truth after it has been sent? The fact is that you are quite aware of the teachings of your Lord. Now, it is your responsibility to pay attention to the wisdom, and the rest will be up to God.

It is only when you actively try to resist the temptations that you are faced with that God will step in, to help you battle the instincts that want to lead you astray. You must place a resolve in your heart to never go against the teachings of God. Righteousness begins by adopting the right intentions. When you are falling into corruption, you might make the mistake of thinking that God is unaware of your actions. You might be blinded by your base instincts, so that good appears to be evil, and evil appears to be good to you. However, if you remove the blinkers that have been put on your eyes, you will realize that you have only been going down a path of iniquity. You are, in fact, doing injustice – to yourself as well as to others. God's wisdom has asked you to open your heart to correction and instruction, which the Lord mercifully sends your way.

It has asked you to become receptive to words of truth that will help you distinguish right from wrong. One of the things that God has taught is the significance of lawful, committed relationships. Such are the relationships that are established to serve God. If you violate the sanctity of the legitimate bonds that are sacred in the eyes of God, you are sure to incur His displeasure.

Your soul cannot bear the consequences of God's disapproval. Thus, avoiding this sin of seducing women can take a more significant toll on your soul than you might realize or admit. It might have consequences worse than you anticipated. You have received your family and friends for comfort and social belonging. The Lord asks you to find comfort and delight in them. Keeping away from the sin of adultery will lead you to live a bountiful life; on the other hand, if you indulge in this life of temptation, you will bring ruin upon yourself. The path of adultery appears to be as shiny as gold, but wisdom tells you that not everything that shines is gold. As far as sins go, seducing other women can quickly become like quicksand. You will sink deeper and deeper, the more time you spend indulging in it.

Soon, you might feel unable to see any light that might guide you out of the darkness that you have fallen into. You will be in a prison of your own making, left without any means to break out of it. This sin might have started off innocently enough. However, rest assured that if you persist in it, you might find yourself chained to live out its consequences for a long time.

Your sins might appear to be innocuous to you. You might feel complacent and feel no remorse or guilt at having done wrong. However, the truth is that such sins feed on you. They eat away at you from the inside till they consume all the good in your soul and become stronger than you are. In time, you will become so weak that you will be on the mercy and whims of your sins. They will control you, and you will feel hollowed out because you disobeyed the explicit instructions of your Lord. No longer will you be able to claim mastery over yourself! You will become a slave to your desires. You see, this sin begins as a form of self-deception. You like those other women. You are enamored of their beauty. You are attracted to them, as surely as a moth is drawn to fire. You want to seduce them because this gives you a sense of pleasure and satisfaction. However, such delights never last for long.

As time passes, you are no longer able to derive as much pleasure and satisfaction out of it as before. Yet, you do not stop acting this way. Do you know why this happens? The reason is this sin evolves into a habit that you cannot let go of. When that happens, you are left with no power to quit, even if you desperately want to.

Do you want to land yourself in such a state where you feel powerless and where you are away from the light of our Lord? The answer is that no one wants that to happen, not if they really think about it. When people get into this sin, they do so with their judgment and better sense, clouded by their carnal desires. However, there is a way out of this predicament that you are caught in. And that way is the one sent to you by God.

Remind yourself that God is watching you wherever you are, and in whatever that you do. When you become so acutely aware of the presence of your Lord, you will feel disinclined to disobey His Word. You would not want to go against His teachings because you put Him first above everything else. The Lord has instructed you to find happiness with your lawful partner so that you are content and happy.

Follow the wisdom that your Lord has shared with you, and you will be at peace, free of the heaviness and darkness of sin. A successful life is one that is lived for the pleasure of the Lord. Though you may be charmed by beautiful figures and faces, you must live a life of faith so that your existence pleases God. This life of faith involves being faithful to your lawful relations and reserving your love only for them.

It directly means avoiding the sin of seducing women because that is certain to lead you away from your Lord. Do not embrace the path of willfulness, for that will only lead to your own downfall. By living a life of self-pleasure, you will form self-destructive habits that will undermine your long-term happiness. You will end up becoming a victim of your own doing. Soon, the pleasure that you might find in immoral acts will wane, but you might find yourself addicted to the sin for no other reason than your consistent pursuit of it. What will you do when such a thing happens? The first step should be to take a step back and reevaluate your life. Remember the wisdom that your Lord has sent to you. Examine yourself honestly and break away from such temptations that may be more than ready to lead you away from your Lord. You must avoid all evil ways.

You can do that by telling yourself that the gratification from your sin will be momentary, but its consequences will surely outlast any pleasure that you may get from it. God has decided a straight and firm path of good for you. Do not fall into temptations that will take you away from the straight path that leads to your Lord. Make sure of that, so your life remains an example of fruitful service to your Lord.

Chapter 6
Financial Wisdom

One of the key facets of wisdom is humbling yourself. In fact, on the path of acquiring wisdom, you must humble yourself, or learning will not be possible. Arrogance will not help you learn and grow in wisdom. A wise man is the one who learns from every source of knowledge available to him.

You see, you must rescue yourself, instead of waiting for someone else to do the job for you. Many people wait around lazily for someone or something to come and do for them what is, in fact, part of their work. They want someone else to induce a change in them and carry them away from the trap of life's evils. The truth is that only you are responsible for turning your life around.

When the Lord asks you to 'deliver' yourself, He wants you to use your faculties to escape the clutches of evil. You must summon up all your energy to save yourself from the risks and dangers that this life poses to a faithful believer. The people who have become wiser move with a sense of urgency to protect themselves from the threats to their faith that lurk at every corner.

An example that our Lord has given to exemplify the significance of hard work is of the ant. You, too, can be instructed by nature if you so desire by observing and pondering upon the life of an ant. A proactive learner of wisdom does not shy away from learning from the humblest of God's creatures. The ant, if you think about, is the perfect example that can teach you valuable lessons.

They do not need any leader to prod it forward. No, an ant takes the initiative itself and gets things done on its own. It is responsible for itself, and it carries that responsibility well enough for the Lord to have recommended it as a model to learn from. Like the ant, you too don't need a supervisor if you are willing to take on the mantle of self-change. You need not put things off till tomorrow that you can do today.

The Lord wants you to give up laziness and be an active participant to bring about the evolution in yourself. You must not delay the task anymore; realize that you already have postponed the right thing for a long time. The more you wait, the more difficult it would seem to you to start your plan of action. It is time that you wake up from the deep slumber that you have fallen into. Your Lord has equipped you with the guidance, as well as the right tools to give yourself the transformation that you require. So now, you must take the first step so that your new life – one marked by wisdom and judiciousness – can start. The Lord also wants you to learn financial wisdom, which refers to wise financial acts that will help you maintain the economic aspect of your life. Consider the example of the ant again. The ant acts preemptively, and during times of abundance, it saves for times when there might be shortfalls.

The ant does not become self-satisfied when it has plenty in the present; instead, it acts in anticipation of the future. It works hard in the present so that its future will be secure. So, save up when you can. Make practical financial choices and do everything at the right time. Do not let laziness stop you from working to safeguard your future.

Remember, diligence and commitments are the keys to improving your life. The Lord has related seven evils that you must avoid if you want to lead a life of virtuousness and righteousness. These sins are a proud look, a lying tongue, a hand that sheds innocent blood, a heart that devised wicked plans, feet that are swift in running to evil, a false witness who speaks lies, and one who sows discord amongst people. These are grave sins that must not be taken lightly.

Wisdom dictates that one refrains from committing any of these sins at all costs. Pride is a sin often mentioned in the scripture as one that has serious consequences. This sin refers specifically to the aspect of conceit or a sense of self-superiority. People who are guilty of this sin look down upon others, but they do not realize that in doing so, they are rebelling against the word of God. It is also common knowledge that Satan was guilty of this sin.

The wise, obviously, would not want to belong to the same category as Satan. If you think about it, all sins can be traced back to this one sin of pride; in other words, pride is the root of evil. Hence, abstain from exalting and praising yourself, for pride is a sin that can erode goodness from you as inevitably as water erodes rock till it turns to dust.

Lying is yet another sin that displeases the Lord, so much so that He warns His believers against it several times. Lying means to communicate falsehood, or to present incorrect information as though it were true. Lying is a form of deception and is a defiant show of disobedience to the word of God. The Lord loves those who tell the truth and are trustworthy. Conversely, He detests those who resort to lying. Not only does lying harm the one listening to it, but it also harms the liar, even though they may think otherwise. A wise man, thus, is the one who refrains from distorting the truth and misinforming others, for that is sure to incur the displeasure of the Lord. Shedding innocent blood is the third sin that the Lord has determined to be deeply grievous. This is a sin that refers to committing a deliberate act of murder – that is, taking away the life of another human being through a conscious effort.

It is a coldblooded deed that takes away an innocent person's right to live. It does not refer to acts of self-defense. When someone commits the murder of an innocent human, they transgress against God because He is the one in whose hands are the decisions of life and death. The Lord has strictly warned believers against this sin; those who do not heed the warning will be severely punished in the afterlife for committing this sin.

Then, the Lord also mentions the person who hatches up devious, wicked plans in the list of sinners whom He detests. These are the people who are scheming and laying down vile plots. They would stop at nothing to get what they want. They use all means possible and always desire to attain their ends by hook or by crook. The Lord considers this as wickedness because it signals moral deprivation and spiritual barrenness in the person who commits this sin. Those guilty of this act have a strong punishment lying in wait for them, for they directly oppose the word of the Lord. Evil is the fourth sin mentioned, and it refers to all actions – committed or thought of – that go against God. Evilness contrasts with righteousness and pious behavior.

There are many ways to commit evil, and those that are evildoers care not for the damage they may cause to others. They wreak havoc in the moral, spiritual, and social fabric of society, as well as in other areas of life. They, therefore, are worthy of fitting retribution at the hands of the Lord, and that is merely just considering how lasting and widespread the consequences of their actions can be.

Being a false witness is another crime that the wise and learned must avoid. This is an act of grave sin whereby a person misrepresents the truth and does so with a sense of impunity, not concerned at all about what would follow from their immoral actions. He or she becomes a false witness when they, with their words, lead people away from the Lord. They may lie, or they may deny the truth that the Lord has sent down. They will be dealt with justly by God because a sinner would only sow what they reap in the end. Sowing discord amongst others is a sin that refers to the act of instigating divisions and starting up quarrels between believing people. The people who are guilty of this sin create discord, which results in ruined relationships and hostility that often has long-term consequences. Such people actively plan to foster disharmony and bring about the destruction that has a ripple effect that impacts individuals, as well as communities.

The Lord has prescribed for the wise to steer clear of these seven sins. He has, additionally, also asked to exercise wisdom when it comes to financial matters and one's future – spiritual, moral, or otherwise. This means becoming an effective believer who, keeping in mind the Lord's guidance, works actively to receive God's approval and love in all matters of life. Such are the people who God holds in His favor and will surely reward.

The Lord sent His commands to guide those who want to be guided. The wise man is guided by the light of wisdom that the Lord has sent down to earth in His infinite mercy. The wise man knows that to defy the wisdom that the Lord has communicated to mankind is akin to harming your own self. A wise man has the understanding that, in the end, it is the soul that is significant over any worldly and earthly luxury and pleasures. And so, he strives with all his might to save his soul for that, which he knows is his true treasure.

Chapter 7
Keep God's Commandments and Live

As you work your way toward acquiring the wisdom that God has sent for you to learn, some things will become apparent to you as daylight. The first of those is that there will be many forces in your life – in the shape of people, work, and other distractions – that will try to lead you away from God.

You might find yourself under a regular assault from such forces that will want to steer you to a different path – a path where there is no light, nor the mercy of your Lord to provide deliverance. Unwittingly, you might fall prey to such suggestions that will take you away from God. These insinuations to disobey God are so quietly whispered in your heart that you do not even realize it till it is too late.

These are the suggestions that plant the seeds of doubt in your heart so that you start to question the things that your heart has faith in. Your job as a person who pursues wisdom faithfully is to remain on guard against all such suggestions that will surely bring about your ruin and downfall.

You must adhere to the words of wisdom that you have heard and received from the Lord. You must not only read those words but implement them in your life. In this way, you can live by the words of wisdom and stay away from deadly sins. You must keep the commandments of God alive in you – and the only way that you can do this is by living your life by them. You must make a commitment to keep away from the invitations of immoral people who would rejoice if you abandoned the straight path.

What would help is becoming a part of a strong community – composed of your family, friends, and the people who you trust. This is what will assist you in remaining steadfast and on the right track. Several times you will be confronted with vile temptations and offers that will tell you to go against the word of God. Do you want to know what will help you remain planted on your feet and not give in to them?

It will only be your will to stay true to your Lord, as well the support of moral people who are with you on your journey to attain wisdom, which can help you remain resolute in your obedience to your Lord. At all times, you must be aware of those who would attempt to smooth talk you into following them and their wicked ways. They will use sweet words to manipulate and misguide you. They intend is to make you follow them on the path of evil and wickedness, which they willfully and diligently stick to. Such are the people who do not care about what ends they might reach due to their defiance of the Lord. You must be conscious of the words of flattery that they are sure to use to trap you.

You must be able to differentiate between truth and falsehood so that you, inadvertently and unknowingly, are not directed toward the wrong path where there is only the displeasure of your Lord waiting for you. Do not pay heed to those people who are blatant about their rebellion and disobedience. These people will loudly declare their intentions of defying the Lord's word.

Moreover, they will ambush those who work in the Lord's way faithfully and who make sacrifices in the service of their Lord. Such people are present at every corner in life. They do not shy away from committing wrongful actions that harm those who believe in the Lord with all their hearts. These evil people are out for vengeance against those who devotedly follow the word of the Lord.

You must be on your guard against such people, for they will surely mislead you into disobedience. You must also remain on guard against liars, who will give you information that has been distorted and mangled to suit their own means. They will pile up lies upon lies so that you believe in their mistruths and veer away from the true path of wisdom. The wise people, however, know what to do under such circumstances.

Divine wisdom demands that you keep your eyes open to distinguish the truth from illusion. Follow the word of God, be open to His loving instructions, and you will be able to overcome the allure of their temptations. You must not listen to people who tempt you through lust and misdirection. They will call you to commit wrong and criminal acts by presenting to you the pleasures of this finite world.

You will be presented with sights that might bedazzle you, for they will be appealing to the eye. You will find many opportunities for satiating yourself through unlawful means. There may be attempts to lull you into a false sense of security by lying to you. You might also be told your actions will have no consequences, and that no one will hold you accountable for them.

However, you know that the Lord watches over what you do. You know that you are answerable to the Lord at every step of the way. Do not yield to such temptations, as they will only lead you to your destruction. These are the sights that may appeal to you. However, giving up and giving in to these suggestions of wrongful acts is analogous to committing a wrong against yourself.

Your life, which you have dedicated to your Lord, is not to be wasted after those who have no love for their Lord. You must take every step to insure yourself against such people, who are out to damage the life of wisdom that you have carefully built. It is, sometimes, so much easier to go after the calls of such people. It takes strong strength of character and moral daring to resist their invitation.

However, remember that you must muster up all your courage to repel such influences from your life, which will only deplete you of righteousness. Following the incitement of such people is akin to going for your own slaughter. The choice is yours to make; will you accept the invitation of the wrongdoers and destroy yourself, or will you stand firm and keep the commandments of God alive in your life? Strengthen your heart so that it does not fall into self-destructive patterns. Do not make wrong decisions that will cost you your whole life. Just ask yourself the question, *"Is that what you have worked so hard for? Can you afford to lose the goodwill of your Lord?"* Most certainly, the answer is in the negative. So, you must train your heart to heed the words of warning. Counsel yourself and others to accept the words of wisdom that the Lord has kindly sent to you, so that you may receive His boundless love and mercy.

There have been many before you who have lost their way after finding it, just because they could not resist the calls of the temptress. Do not be one of those people. What is sadder than to lose wisdom, after you have found it? Save yourself from the dire consequences that will follow all acts of sins and wrongdoings. Become strong so that you can fend off the attacks of the wrongdoers. You will see that the rewards of doing so will be manifold and will make it all worth it in the end.

Chapter 8
Listen to Wisdom

There are more benefits to be had from wisdom than you might realize at first. Not only does wisdom keep you away from the anger of God, but it also provides you with all kinds of riches in life. Wisdom to a believer is like the call of a bird to a lost traveler. You will be led to the elixir of life if you follow the calls of wisdom, for it is the only thing that will remove all ills and evils from your life.

Wisdom is calling out to each and every single human being, regardless of where they stand in life. Even so, there aren't many who have their ears open to this sweet voice that will lead them to redemption. Most people have become deaf to the voice of wisdom; they just don't listen to it though it is right there, waiting to help them out of their problems.

So, what will it take for you to remove the mufflers that you have knowingly or unknowingly put over your ears that do not allow you to listen to wisdom? Wisdom stands at the rise of the road. It waits for you at the crossroads of life, ready to tell you the right direction if you are lost – but are you open to receiving guidance? Wisdom takes her stand next to the gates of the city, and then she cries out for people to pay heed before time runs out for them. Yet, how many are there who truly listen to the words that wisdom sends out their way daily without fail? Those people are in ever-dwindling numbers. Wisdom says, *"People, I call out to you! My cry is to mankind, so that they may listen and learn. O you simple ones! Will it not be in your benefit to understand and be prudent? Open yourself up to my words so you may receive the grace of God. Be of an understanding heart. Listen to me, for I speak only of excellent things that will take you to your Lord."*

Every word of wisdom that you will hear is instructive. It is educational, and it will help you better yourself and gain status in the sight of your Lord. Do you know why? It is because wisdom never lies; it never falsifies things by making ugly things beautiful for your eyes. Wickedness is an abomination to Wisdom's heed. Everything that wisdom tells you is steeped in righteousness. If wisdom is a tree, then, righteousness is its water and its sunlight; it is the source of its growth. Wisdom is the antidote to the ill of crookedness and perverseness. This is the truth that appears plain and pure before the eyes of the one who pays heed.

The heedless ones, however, are unable to see the truth that burns as bright as the sun in the skies. The former are the people who travel the path of knowledge to reach the ultimate destination, which is their Lord; the latter are those who are led astray, who forever remain lost and can never come close to their journey's end, though they may travel their entire lives.

Wisdom says, *"Receive my instruction for it is better than silver and diamonds. Verily, knowledge is above the choicest gold. And I, wisdom, am better than the reddest rubies in the world. All the things you may desire cannot be compared with me, for I am the most worthy out of all of them. I am the one that will last when the others will fall prey to Time."* This has always proven to be true – you may look for the riches of this world, but they can never be equal to wisdom in any way. This is because wisdom is the treasure that lasts when all else perishes with time.

Wisdom dwells in prudence. Prudence means to fear incurring the displeasure of your Lord. This fear of the Lord is what makes a believer hate evil, pride, arrogance, and all the immoral ways of the world that tempt a believer away from the straight path. There will be mouths that will spout perverse things, but will you listen to their words, or will you listen to the words of wisdom? The choice is yours to make. Knowledge and discretion are the byproducts of wisdom. Once you reach out to the source of wisdom, you will become knowledgeable beyond your expectations. If there is one thing that has had an impact throughout the centuries, it is wisdom.

Kings and rulers are amongst those who have listened to the counsel of wisdom and have benefited by it. In fact, all the judges of the earth have relied on wisdom to make justice the way of the world. Wisdom is readily available to the common man as well. To you and me, and to everyone willing to receive it, wisdom calls out expressively.

Wisdom says, *"I love those who love me, and those who seek me diligently will find me."* By this, it becomes apparent that to get wisdom, you must first seek it actively. Wisdom comes to those who are not passive; it comes to those who have a love of it and are willing to go to some lengths and work hard to acquire it. Wisdom says, *"Riches and honor are with me. Lasting wealth and righteousness are also with me."* This means that those who look for these things elsewhere are searching in vain. There is one source of riches and honor, wealth and righteousness – and that is wisdom. It brings justice and virtue. It gives a man those treasures that will outlast this mortal world and their earthly existence. On the other hand, worldly assets will succumb to the ravages of time and be lost. They will not come to your aid when you need them – the only thing that will help you, by being your guide and your rescuer, is wisdom. Wisdom says, *"The Lord made me at the beginning of His creation."*

This means that wisdom precedes man. It has been there before, and it will be there after him. Wisdom was created before the bounties of this earth were marked. It was sent down the skies like rain; it was delivered before the hills and mountains were established on this earth. It came before earth's soil and the sky.

Wisdom was there before the oceans were filled up to the brim, before limits were set on them, and before the foundations of the earth were laid. Wisdom was present to rejoice in all the creations of the Lord. It saw its role as the guide, and to this day, it continues to help those who wish to be helped on their way to the Lord. Wisdom wants all the faithful to be wise and to listen to the instructions that it imparts.

If you ignore the calls of wisdom and choose to disregard its warnings, you will exchange losses for gains. On the other hand, if you listen to wisdom, not only will you be happier and more abundant in all the ways that matter, but you will also get closer to your Lord and be rewarded with His mercy and grace.

Chapter 9
Wisdom, not Foolishness

After having learned of wisdom, is there anyone who would still choose foolishness over it? Is there anyone who would select loss over gain, who would exchange satisfaction for pain? The truth is that those who become open to wisdom experience their heart blossoming like flowers to receive the love and mercy of their Lord. Their hearts, as a result, become capable of differentiating between right and wrong, and between what will benefit them and what will destroy them.

The ways of the foolish are strange. The dumb man persists in everything that he does, with the flawed belief that he is right. He is wise in his own eyes. The truth, even though it may burn as bright as fire, will elude him for his eyes have been covered by blinkers that prevent him from seeing the reality for what it is. In other words, a fool is confident of his stupid ways so much so that he rants and rages self-righteously, even though he does wrong things. A fool is reckless and impatient: he wants things when he wants them, and for this reason, he would sacrifice his long-term benefit for the sake of short-term pleasure. A fool proudly follows the wrong crowd and indulges in wrongful acts until they become a way of life for him. He might do so without being disturbed by any sense of guilt. However, wisdom has informed everyone that the consequences of one's actions will always catch up with them in the end. The fool can run fast, and he can run far, but never can he run fast enough or far enough to evade the results of his wrongful acts, born out of foolishness.

Foolishness can stick to a man like the thickest glue. However, with will and wisdom, one can rid themselves of foolishness. Then again, there are those who have decided in their hearts never to change their ways, and so they will remain foolish to the end. They will gladly go down the path of evil that will lead them to the destination of destruction. They will do so willingly, convinced of being right when they are anything but.

Foolishness leads to ruin – and that is as certain to happen, as it is for day to follow night. Foolishness leads a man down, twisting roads that get him nowhere. The foolish man relies upon his heart and then decides. He fails to see that the heart might be under the assault of temptations, that it might prefer immorality over righteousness, and that the heart is fallible and is susceptible to sins. Wisdom, on the other hand, is from the Lord. A man of wisdom is a man of understanding. So, while the foolish man indulges in sport, the wise man has the acumen to rise above the pettiness of life and do such things that would take him to his Lord. Wisdom is what leads to deliverance, while foolishness only leads to damnation.

While foolishness turns a man away from good, wisdom turns him away from evils and the losses that come with it. Wisdom teaches a man to think about and consider all the steps that he may take in life. Foolishness, on the other hand, makes him rush into the wrong things. Wisdom instructs man to pay attention to wise counsel that will always show him light when he is surrounded by darkness.

Foolishness, however, will insist that a man disregard all wise advice and do as he pleases – eventually, this is what will lead to his disgrace and downfall. Foolishness blinds man to the truth of God. Wisdom, in contrast, opens his eyes as well as his heart to his Lord. The foolish man falls into committing wrongful deeds that take him ever more away from redemption. The wise man, however, lives a life of righteousness. The foolish man does not recognize his own Creator, while the wise man knows his Lord and is quick to obey His commandments. The foolish man will question and have only disdain for the Lord's Word; however, a wise man will have a love for the Word of God and will always worship Him without rebellion. Wisdom makes a man want to know his God more. Consequently, a wise man would spend his time wisely in contemplation of important matters.

Conversely, foolishness leads only to waste – of time, energy, and other such resources that the Lord has granted to mankind. A foolish man, thus, will forfeit all the good that he has been given for nothing. A wise man would be prudent and will make use of all the spiritual opportunities that a foolish man will only waste happily, staying blissfully unaware of the consequences that will catch up with him in due time.

Wisdom teaches a man to serve God alone. It tells them how brief their time on earth is, and how they must make the most of it by committing himself to the Lord. A heart that has gained in wisdom knows that death awaits all, and so, it rushes to accumulate righteous deeds. On the other hand, a foolish heart lives like there is no tomorrow and indulges in acts that are no good to him or to others. It is obvious who will be better off when all is said and done. Wisdom also allows man to learn the importance of planning out his life so that it follows the right path. A wise man knows that he must work tirelessly to attain spiritual progress, which isn't easy and is, in all ways, hard-won. A foolish man, however, wastes all his days in empty pursuits that amount to nothing in the long run. A wise man understands that the sacrifices he makes for the sake of his Lord will have higher returns than he imagined at the outset of his journey.

Contrary to this, a foolish man chases short-lived pleasures instead of working to attain eternal good. He will go down a road of wastefulness, where he will submit the control of his being to evilness. He will become a perpetrator of evil, thereby tightening the noose around his own neck. It is quite clear what the better choice is. Now the question that arises is, are you willing to make the right decision?

Foolishness will make you carry on with your wild ways. It will make you give in to the temptation to sin. It will lead you to drink wine, seduce women, and live thoughtlessly. It will lead you down a road from where it might be hard to return. Wisdom, on the other hand, will take your hand when you are lost and carry you toward the light. It will help you when you need help and will lovingly bring you toward the Lord's mercy and grace. Wisdom will help you stay away from evil and the foolishness of sin. It will protect you from a life of temptation. It will keep you away from the evils of alcohol, from dishonesty, and from anything that takes you away from your Lord.

So, make the decision now to lead a life like sages rather than like fools. Do not become trapped in the web of evil, for it will draw you in like a spider so that you cannot escape. Live wisely for wisdom is what the Lord has taught us. Do not fall into the wrong ways, which will lead you to Satan and not to God.

Wisdom is what will help you understand God's will. It will light up your path, so you don't stumble and fall as you make your way toward your destiny. Avoid foolishness, for it will impoverish you, spiritually and in other ways. Learn the insight that comes with wisdom, so you are well-equipped to live your life in a way that will please your Lord.

Chapter 10
Wise Instruction from Solomon

Solomon taught that a wise child makes his father glad, but a foolish son only earns grief for his mother. You have read about wisdom enough to know that it is wise to choose righteousness over wickedness. While the former would yield treasures in this world and the next, the latter can only lead to a loss that will last forever.

The Lord always differentiates between the righteous and the wicked, no matter what. He never allows the righteous to go hungry or without that which he needs. On the other hand, He withholds from the wicked what he yearns for. It is only the wise who understands the importance of doing things on time.

A sagacious man knows he must work today so that he is secure tomorrow. It is only foolish who waits till the last day and sleeps at the time of harvest; the result is that he suffers. Not only does the foolish suffer, but he also brings disgrace to his loved ones. It can be said that the wise man has an open heart that is receptive to wisdom, while the foolish man has closed his heart to everything sensible.

A wise man makes the decision to live a life of integrity. He understands the word of his Lord and is determined to live his life by it. On the other hand, the foolish man always sets himself up to live a life of dishonor. And whose life is more secure of the two? The righteous person will always be blessed, but the wicked one will only experience gradual decay.

There is no way for the wicked to hide his true nature. It will become apparent to the world because of his corrupt ways that cannot be concealed, though the wicked man might try to camouflage his true self. Whenever the righteous person speaks, people listen. This is because his words come forth from a well of wisdom. In contrast, a fool's speech is one that will bring destruction to any who follows his words.

Not only is a fool's speech devoid of sense, but it is also one that leads to ruin – his own as well as of others. The wisest man is the richest for his wealth is his wisdom and subsequent knowledge. The foolish man is poor, for he has no wisdom, which is the only valuable treasure to have in this world. The righteous man is wise because he knows he must follow his Lord's instructions.

On the contrary, a foolish man goes against the guidance of his Lord. In the end, he suffers the consequences of it. As the wise man will speak kind words, the foolish will speak words of lies and hatred and wouldn't stop short of spreading slander. The speeches of the wise and the foolish reflect the contrasting states of their heart. Wise is the man who can control his speech, for it is only the foolish man who never thinks before he speaks. The speech of the foolish man will reveal the rotten condition of his heart.

The heart of the wise and righteous person is of profound value to the Lord. As for the foolish and wicked man, his heart and tongue are worthless – not just for this world but for the Lord as well. What a fool does not realize is that his tongue slowly leads him to a life of ruin. The wise man understands that following the Word of his Lord brings value to his life and an everlasting reward. The foolish man does not realize that his loss is eternal and will outlive his life on this earth. It is only in time that it will become apparent that the consequences of our actions, whether righteousness and wickedness, will outlast the life on earth. The righteous person understands that he will be granted the final reward, one that would last forever.

The righteous man's desires and wishes will be allowed to him by the Lord, but the foolish man will have his existence, and all his hoarding goes in vain. The righteous man is the one who knows that fear of the Lord is what extends his life. It is what makes his life rich and worthy, for he gains the favor of the Lord. The righteous person only gains joy from following the Word of his Lord.

The wise man has a safe refuge in the ways of the Lord. On the other hand, the wicked and foolish will be left uprooted from their life as they have deviated from the word of the Lord. The wicked man has a perverse tongue out of which comes only lies and instruments of evil. He is mired in sin and does nothing to change and adopt the ways of the Lord. The righteous man, on the other hand, speaks only wise words.

He does not lack in wisdom; and so, he understands the everlasting benefit that is to be had from earning God's pleasure. The fool, on the contrary, will be only left with regrets, for he does not realize the bargain of loss he makes in the world. Thus, choose wisdom over foolishness and righteousness over wickedness; the reward of the right choice will far outlive the short-term pleasure of the wrong one. Do not be ruined by misinformation that will lead you down a path of foolishness, for it will bring you to your downfall. Always seek refuge in your Lord, for it is only by His Grace that you can have a well-lived existence.

Chapter 11
Dishonesty Does Not Pay

The wise man knows the worth of honesty. He also knows that while being dishonest, he would not stand a chance with his Lord, for the Lord knows all the ways of dishonesty. The Lord hates the use of dishonest scales. On the other hand, the Lord loves honest and truthful dealings. There is nothing but the fear of the Lord in the heart of the righteous man, which keeps him living a life of integrity and worthiness. On the other hand, the foolish man overlooks the instructions of the Lord and dooms himself in his willful blindness.

The wise man has learned humbleness. As he knows humility, he finds favor with his Lord. Then there are the dishonest people who go about life, rebelliously disregarding the Word of God. They adopt deceitful methods; what they don't realize is that in doing so, they only harm themselves ultimately. While the righteous person benefits from his wisdom, the wicked just reaps the punishment for his own foolish ways. The wise man will be delivered, but the wicked one will only fall victim to his contriving.

It is only a fact that the righteous man will outlive his earthly existence by earning the pleasure of the Lord. However, a wicked man will perish once he breathes his last on earth. The hopes of the righteous man yield the rewards that he has wanted, but the wishes of the wicked man will go unfulfilled, for the Lord does not hold the wicked in His favor. The wicked man places his hopes in his worldly riches.

What he does not realize is that these are fragile means that will perish. These are not the things that will earn him the favor of his Lord. On the contrary, the righteous man understands the precariousness of such temporary things, and so, he places his hopes with his Lord, who then delivers him from death and despair. The wicked man falls into the same trap that the Lord saves the righteous from. It is clear who earns loss and who gathers gains after this mortal life.

The wise man is the one who lives a life of honor. His existence is upright, and so, he follows the word of his Lord. He loves his neighbor and takes care so that no harm comes to his neighbor from his hand. He knows how to hold peace. On the other hand, the wicked man has not learned his Lord's instructions, so he lives his life in disobedience.

For this reason, he brings harm to his neighbor and exacerbates conflicts. Not only that, but the wicked man rejoices in hurting the dignity of his neighbor. The righteous person will be saved from the harm that the wicked man would want to inflict upon him only by the grace of God. The wise man also understands the importance of keeping secrets. The foolish man, on the contrary, has a loose tongue: he will reveal all, even the things he was trusted with in confidence.

A foolish man will be happy to gossip, for he sees no harm in doing so. A wise man, however, understands that what people need is counsel, rather than gossip-mongering. He will then share words of wisdom instead of speaking ill of everything and everyone.

The wise and righteous man will do his best to provide his counsel; one that is in line with the word of the Lord. The wise man will earn reward not only for himself but will also provide benefit to those that he gives good counsel to. In that way, he will earn even more reward. The righteous man takes the straight path, whereas the foolish man perishes on the road of wickedness. What the foolish man does not realize is that he is only harming his own flesh and soul. He is the one who will be burdened by the sins that he has committed in this world. The Lord holds righteousness in high esteem, but He despises the wicked and foolish for the ways they fall into. The wicked man only deceives himself into thinking that his actions will not be accounted for. All his actions will be tallied, and he will then suffer punishment for his wrongdoing.

It is divine wisdom which declares that the hopes of the righteous are good, while the desires of the wicked are harmful. Who, then, is the richer of the two? The wise man will always be at an advantage over the foolish man who only makes transactions of eternal losses. Wisdom says that anyone who puts his trust in the wealth of the world is the ultimate loser.

It is only the person who trusts his Lord, who wins in the end. The righteous person will be successful while the foolish will only land in trouble, for that is all he sets himself up for. The wise man will bring honor to himself as well as his family, but the wicked man will only gather shame and disgrace for the entire community. The former earns the favor of his Lord while the other loses the favor that he could have earned.

This is the way of the Lord, who has decided to reward the wise and punish the wicked for their actions in the world. It is true that both the righteous and the foolish shall be repaid for what they do in this world. While the virtuous will be given the fruits of their righteousness, the iniquitous will reap the misfortunes that they have earned through their disobedience to the Lord.

Chapter 12
Whoever Loves Discipline Loves Knowledge

It is the way of the wise to love knowledge. What is wisdom, but the desire to act on the newfound knowledge and learn more? On the other hand, a foolish man will renounce the pursuit of knowledge in favor of remaining ignorant. Thus, one of the primary differences between the wise and the foolish men is that the former loves knowledge while the latter hates any and all corrective measures.

The wise man understands that the Lord will approve of his love for knowledge. He understands that the search for knowledge, which leads to wisdom, is what elevates him in the sight of his Lord. He also knows that it is through the knowledge that he can secure the favor of his Lord, who is Just and All-Seeing.

On the other hand, the foolish man condemns himself by his hatred of knowledge. Then, a wicked man has intentions that are wicked – ones that bring no one any benefit. An example of this is a wise wife who brings honor to her family, while the wicked one brings only shame and disgrace.

The righteous man has only good thoughts that are fair and just. They help him as well others by being a source of guidance. However, the words of the wicked can only lead to ruin and destruction. There are others in the world who will also recognize the merits of the wise man. So, whosoever is wise, he will have a good reputation owing to his wisdom. On the other hand, the foolish man will be despised for his destructive ways that ruin all that appears in their path.

Wisdom tells the wise man that it is better to forego material wealth and have high esteem and a good heart. A wise man is the one who cares for every living being, even the animals. He does no harm to anyone and always strives to be fair and gentle. The wicked and foolish man, on the other hand, will not shy away from being cruel to those around him.

A wicked man does not care for the consequences of his actions, and so, he does as he pleases, not caring about who he hurts in the process. Even those acts that the wicked man thinks are merciful are wicked, for they always produce more harm than good. A wicked man will always choose ill-judgment over good sense. He will desire material riches over spiritual wealth. On the other hand, a wise man will know the true worth and value of the things the wicked man chases after. A wise man will sow seeds that will give him the ultimate reward – that of his Lord's favor. And so, a wise man will always work hard and receive due returns for an obedient existence. The wicked man does not realize the trap that he sets for himself through his own tongue. He transgresses against the limits prescribed by the Lord, and in doing so, he chains himself to face the consequences of his defiance.

The wise man, however, will only be rewarded by the words of his mouth and the work of his hand. While the wicked man will be left dissatisfied, the wise man will be satiated from the rewards that he will have earned through his righteous deeds. The foolish man never looks at himself in the mirror; he is never a fool in his own eyes.

He does not heed the counsel of the wise and goes about living life on his own whims and desires. In doing so, he walks blindly down the path of self-destruction. A foolish man is also one who never tries to moderate his emotional expressions. However, a wise man will hide even his displeasure, if that is what the divine wisdom dictates. A wise man speaks the truth and only gives true testimonies.

On the other hand, a wicked man will not stop twisting the words of truth and giving false witness accounts. There is a tendency toward deceit in the wicked man, and he acts on it without restraint, not heeding the consequences that would soon follow. So, while the words of the wicked man will hurt like lashes, the words of the wise man will be like oil that would soothe those who listen to him speak.

A wicked man will be inclined to commit evil, for sin has taken root in his heart. He doesn't think twice before committing acts of deceit and betrayal, for to him, they are small actions. On the other hand, the righteous man is filled with the grace of God and will only commit activities that bring peace and joy to others. The wise person will not boast of his knowledge though he certainly knows more than the foolish.

He will wait for the right time to speak and use his knowledge to help others. The fool, on the other hand, will brag and be overconfident, and therein lies his fault. In the end, though, he will suffer from the consequences of his arrogance and will be shown for what he truly is. The Lord considers the truthful and honest people as worthy of His utmost favor. Wise is the man who sets his sights on earning the approval of his Lord. In his wisdom, he will only keep a company that takes him closer to his Lord. The fool, on the other hand, will go down the path of wickedness. It is only wise to understand the word of the Lord and then live your life by it, for it will earn you the grace of Lord.

Chapter 13
A Wise Child Responds to His Father's Discipline

Wisdom makes one open – that is, receptive – to receiving more wisdom. So, if a wise child's father admonishes or disciplines him, he will not balk at it. Instead, he would see the wisdom that underlies those acts of discipline. On the other hand, a foolish child would take discipline at face value; and so, he will react against it and refuse to be corrected on his mistakes.

Another fundamental difference between a wise and faithful, and a foolish and unfaithful person is this; the latter is fed by the violence that he relishes, while the former is nourished by the fruits of his faith. The wise person makes it his foremost duty to watch his speech.

He does not speak negatively or needlessly. The foolish person does the exact opposite: his speech is damaging and purposeless. Thereby, a foolish person earns nothing at all, for his acts just bring harm to him as well as others. A wise man, however, earns his rewards in full and is satisfied by his Lord.

The wise man despises lies, so he never lies; the foolish man, on the other hand, lies through his teeth and ends up in disgraceful situations because of this. It is true that the acts of the faithful, as well as the wicked, earn them appropriate rewards. While the wise man's faith brings him his Lord's favor, the wicked man's sins bring him ruination and humiliation. The wicked man can live under the pretense of being rich in the world; the truth, however, remains that the wicked man is at a loss, for his riches are for naught. The wise man is richer, for he has the truest wealth of all wisdom.

The wise man's wisdom shines brighter than the foolish man's errands. The wicked man is self-important, for he is blinded to the truth of his actions. However, his arrogance only lands him in conflicts and arguments. A wise man, on the other hand, learns and takes advice. He will become all the wealthier for it because when he seeks advice from those who are wiser, he increases his wisdom. This wealth of the wise is hard-won, for it comes through labor and dedicated efforts. Hard work and diligence go into making his wealth last; not only that, but they help the wise one multiply his wealth. On the contrary, the foolish man's wealth is obtained through deception and deceit.

As such, his wealth only diminishes as time passes, though he may be too misguided to see the truth for what it is. The foolish man treats all instructions with contempt and disdain. He does not realize that he will, ultimately, pay the price for his offensive behavior. On the other hand, it is the wise man who always pays heed; he listens to competent counsel and is duly rewarded for it. The wise man also knows wisdom to be the fountain of life. As such, he drinks from this fountain and consequently can avoid the pitfalls that lay in wait for human beings. The wise man is saved by his faith and wisdom.

The wise man has the common sense that the foolish man doesn't. As a result, he lives a life of grace. The wicked man who has no faith also has no sense. For this reason, he treads a difficult path in life. He doesn't know right from wrong, and as he eschews instruction, he doesn't learn to differentiate between truth and falsehood. The mark of a faithful man is his knowledge and wisdom; the sign of a wicked man is his foolishness that shows in his every word and action. The wise man lives a wholesome life of faith. However, the evil man, in time, becomes a victim of his own foolishness; he falls into adversity, and one that lasts a lifetime and beyond. It is a fact that the one who does not pay heed falls into shame and disgrace. This is merely a product of his ignorance; it is because he refuses to listen to the instruction that he remains stuck in this cycle of wickedness. He doesn't realize that decline awaits him. His bankruptcy is both spiritual and worldly, for he loses everything when all is said and done. On the contrary, a wise man doesn't shy away from education and improvement. It is for this reason that he will be honored and held in favor of his Lord.

A wise man knows that his company not only affects him but also defines him as an individual. For this reason, he keeps company with the wise and the faithful. The foolish man, however, will be a companion to fools; he would shun the company and guidance of wise men, for he refuses to benefit from their wise counsel.

The wicked man resists all attempts at education, and clings to evil; he is the poorer for it, but he does not see it. In the end, the wise man earns rewards, while the foolish man only accumulates loss. While disaster befalls the wicked, the faithful are saved by the grace of the Lord. The wise man can leave his inherited wealth to his progeny; on the other hand, the wealth of the wicked man will only, by the will of the Lord, find its way to the wise man. In this way, the wicked are never able to enjoy the fruits of his supposed wealth, for the Lord does not deem him fit to receive rewards from Him. The Lord has decreed that the righteous are destined for good, while the wicked are fated to live a life of loss.

The wise man knows this, and so, he not only receives discipline but also hands out discipline to his child, for he knows it will only benefit him. Thus, the righteous, through openness to wisdom, earn their due reward, while the wicked people remain empty-handed till the end.

Chapter 14
A Wise Woman Builds

A wise woman is the one who lives with the fear of God. She shapes her life around the dictation laid down by the Lord and lives by the guidance presented down to her; she knows that her salvation is in following the Lord's word. Such a woman builds her house, and this house is full of the Lord's favor and blessings. On the contrary, a foolish woman takes apart the bricks of her own house; she does this because she has little regard for the teachings of the Lord. She willfully sins and does wrong. In the end, she only brings shame and disgrace, not just on herself but her family.

A wise person is an honest witness. He doesn't lie for he knows the value of honesty; so, he despises dishonesty and works hard to build an upright character. A wicked person, on the other hand, has no faith; wisdom eludes him for she mocks the righteous and their moral ways of living. The wise person finds wisdom and knowledge, for she is made more perceptive by the grace of the Lord. Staying away from the foolish person is vital, for one learns nothing but stupidity from them.

All a foolish person imparts is idiocy, and all she shows is a willingness to sin. This is because a foolish woman knows no better. The foolish woman does not know that if he makes a mockery of sin, and indulges in it time and again, it will come back to haunt him in the future. He will be met with disappointment and disrepute, for that is the just compensation of all his actions. The sensible person, on the other hand, lives a life of the Lord's favor. He will have a prosperous life because he is blessed by his Lord. The house of the faithful, wise man, thrives, for he has the Lord's favor.

The house of the wicked, however, is destined to be demolished, for he earns only the Lord's wrath. In their hearts, both the evil and the righteous know their fate. The wicked might pretend to be better off in his wicked ways, but his heart finds no joy; his happiness fades, and his success evaporates for they are not lasting. The wise, however, has other righteous people to share in his happiness. This way, the joys and blessings of the wise and virtuous man multiplies, while those of the wicked man diminish and vanish. A foolish man finds no lasting happiness for his heart is aware of the ultimate destruction that awaits him.

Even the delight of a foolish man will end in sorrow; he goes against the teachings of the Lord and gets fitting repayment for his disobedience. A foolish man never learns to mend his ways and is regretful at the end of his life; this is because he believed the wicked and lost his chance to earn his Lord's favor. Contrary to this, a wise man finds satisfaction in his Lord's Word. He likes wisdom and is watchful of every word that he is exposed to; this is the reason why the wise man is protected from the wicked man's speech – because his wisdom is his shield against every rebellious and wicked act that will earn him his Lord's displeasure.

Wisdom helps a person stay away from the ways of evil and wickedness. A wise man is cautious and watches his steps, lest he falls into the temptations of disobedience and sinning. The foolish woman, however, is so prideful of the foolish ways that she stumbles into sin willingly. She is boastful about his sins; she is so brash that he engages in sin without worrying about its evitable consequences that will ultimately bring her downfall. The foolish person is also quick to give in to anger. She reveals his foolishness through his words and actions. The wicked man, sooner or later, exposes himself. Thus, she gathers scorn and hatred for the malice of her actions, as others recognize him for who she is. The wise man will receive knowledge. The wicked will yield to the righteous; the latter has wisdom and knowledge, which makes him superior to the wicked, foolish person. Wisdom tells the righteous man to love his neighbor, and so, he does. As a result, the wise man lives a happy life – one that is filled with cordiality and warmth.

The wise man has mercy in his heart; he does not scorn the poor and the needy. Thus, he does good deeds for the mere reason of earning his Lord's favor; as in time, his good returns to him in different forms. The wise man earns loyalty and friendliness of the people around him. He benefits others, and so, he gets benefited in return.

The crown of the wise man is his wisdom. It is his best asset and resource, for it continues to benefit without drying up. Wisdom only increases, as it is blessed by the Lord. The foolish man, on the other hand, multiplies just his foolishness. A wise man learns to speak only the truth while the foolish man does not hesitate to lie and deceive. The wise man has a fear of the Lord in his heart, which keeps him away from sins and wrongdoing. The foolish man, however, disregards the guidance provided to him by the Lord and continues to go down the path of recklessness and ruin. The wise man earns grace and peace, which his children inherit. The foolish man earns disgrace, which he then transfers to his children. A wise man is also patient and understanding. He does not rush to act but takes time to measure his thoughts and actions. The foolish man, on the other hand, will react without thought and consideration.

A wise man is calm and cool; a foolish man harbors dark thoughts of jealousy and anger in his heart and suffers much due to them. In time, the wise man feels grace and guiding light in his being. A foolish man, on the other hand, feels the heavyweight of condemnation, for his heart and soul have become corrupt and rotten as he disregarded the Lord's word.

A wicked man's sins are his downfall. A righteous man's integrity is his deliverance. A foolish man loses all hope, for he did not place his trust in his Lord, but blindly followed the evil's invitations to sin. A wise man, however, feels the warmth of hope, for he always had faith in his Lord and so is saved by His mercy. Even in death, the wise man is happy, for he has faith that his Lord will save him from damnation.

The foolish man, however, finds no rest, for he has only earned loss upon loss, by not heeding the word of the Lord.

Chapter 15
A Soft Answer Turns Away Wrath

"A gentle answer turns away wrath, but a harsh word stirs up anger"

-Proverb 15:1

A soft answer is often the source of melting down a hardened heart. It all depends on our words, as there is a saying which states that *"It is not about what you say, it is about how you say it."* It is the words that we say or mean that sow the seeds of either happiness or sadness in people. If we speak softly and gently, it will definitely turn away God's wrath from us and allow us to understand the problems of people around us.

We need to humble ourselves because it is what Jesus Christ has taught us too. Therefore, if we follow His instructions of being a humble and polite person, we would be able to turn away God's anger that we might have earned in the past. The chapter illustrates the differences between wise men and foolish ones.

It speaks about the words of the wiser ones which only deliver the truth or talk about knowledge. Nothing that they speak out from their mouths is witless. However, on the other hand, the foolish person would always speak out folly, and words that are egregious and cut right through the soul. The words that are spoken by the wise ones give happiness and are soothing to the soul. But when the foolish speaks, it always harms the listeners because his words often damage the inner instincts that are present in all people.

There are obviously two kinds of people in the world, the good and the bad ones. Therefore, we should not think that whatever we do or say is not under the watchful eye of God. In fact, His eyes roam over the world, and they keep in the notice, the virtue and the vice that is being done by His people. Nothing can escape His strict watch.

The mouth of the wise spreads love and life among people who listen to them. Their words can become the tree of life, as mentioned in the Book of Proverbs, Chapter 15. Whereas on the other hand, when an evil or unwise person speaks out, they are unable to spread love, instead they spread hatred. Their words crush the soul as if there are thousands of knives cutting through it, as their speech acts just like a slashing blade. When it comes to the offspring of the wise and evil, there is a comparison between them as well. The unwise person would always scorn away the teachings of his parents. Now, this could happen in two ways. The foolish one would despise the instructions of his parents, even if he knows that they are beneficial for him, which means he is also aware of the consequences. Or, in the other case, the fool would unknowingly avoid the directions of his parents, which can also be harmful to him in the same manner.

He would always loathe his father's discipline. Whereas, the wise one would always listen to what his parents are instructing him about, and so would earn happiness and wellbeing in the future. He would always accept correction from not only his parents but also from other elders. And so, in this way, he would be able to please God.

Let us talk about the house and possessions of the wise and the evil. The Bible says that the home of a wise man would always be filled with his bounty and that his treasures will be full. Whereas on the other hand, the fool's money will always bring adversities and disasters. The wealth of the wise is always blessed because he earns it with God-fearing intentions.

However, as whatever the fool earns is always without the heavenly consent, at the end of the day, there is a possibility that he might lose it all in exchange for some vice. The fool's wealth is without the blessings of God; therefore, it tends to bring curse or unfavorable situations for him. The wise man would always speak the truth because he lives his life with the knowledge of the judgment day since he knows that everything that he says or does is answerable to God at Doom's Day. But the fools are always running away from the path of righteousness and so are away from God.

The Book of Wisdom states that *"The sacrifice of the wicked is detestable to the Lord, but the prayer of the upright pleases Him."* It is evident from this verse that whatever the foolish ones bring forth to the altar of the Lord as a sacrifice is detested and suspected by God because He knows that the sacrifice of the fool has not been earned by lawful means. But the sacrifice that is brought by the righteous is accepted by God, with its sweet-smelling aroma that reaches the heavens with acceptance from God. Discipline is harsh for the people who go astray from the path of righteousness. If you hate correction, you will not be able to live your life to the fullest, and the end result of which will be death ultimately. Whatever the humans do is open to the eyes of the Lord for which He will reward and punish us all. God also owns heaven and hell; therefore, death and destruction are also open to Him. She'ol is a place that is reserved for the dead and where the wicked will be dwelling. This will be the place for the abandoned souls, as they will have to go to the abyss to face the eternal punishment held by God.

Those who make fun of the instructions bring the wrath of God unto themselves. He sees them all and notices their actions. Such people are fools who mock corrections, which is why they always stay away from the wiser people. A foolish person does not like being corrected, which is why he would refuse to go to the wise for advice.

Those who have a happy soul are happy from within, especially within their souls. And when they are happy, it is shown from their facial expressions as well because their happiness is genuine. If the heart and the soul are happy, it will be obvious on your face as well. However, sadness can crush one's soul and may occur because of dumb choices and staying away from the word of the Lord. He who wants to get knowledge and is after every chance to obtain it is the one who never misses an opportunity to get the information.

He is always seeking knowledge from all resources. But the fool, on the other hand, would always feed on foolishness. Those who are oppressed will have miserable days. The troubled souls will get to face sorrows for long. But those who are happy with God will enjoy elongated happiness. It is better to have fewer things in your possession that you need, rather than having something that is not yours.

Own things with the fear of God in your heart because they stay with you for longer. But the things that have not been owned under God's supervision are all temporary. Similarly, it is better to have a simple meal that is filled with love, rather than having lavish dinners that are filled with hatred, agony, and falsehood. A person who is short-tempered and loses his cool sooner always becomes the reason for tantrums and fights.

Whereas a calm and sober person is always there to settle down a quarrel. The way of a lazy and lethargic person is full of thorns that represent hurdles and obstacles in his life. Whereas, the path of the righteous leads to the highway. A wise child brings peace to his parents by following their instructions in his life. Whereas, a foolish person completely dislikes his mother and her teachings. Insensible people will find joy and happiness in their foolish deeds. But a sensible person always follows the straight path that leads to righteousness and strong virtues. If your plans fail to succeed in your life, this means that they were planned without the consent of any counselor. When the plans are made singlehandedly, they often happen to fail. But when there is the guidance of many counselors available for you, there is a possibility that you get things done the right way.

You will feel happy when an appropriate answer will be delivered by you. And this would become more joyous when that reply is given at the right moment to the right person. The path on which the righteous walks leads upward to heaven so that they do not go down to hell. Wisdom says that God does not stand arrogant people, and He will tear down the house of the proud ones.

Whereas, he promises to establish a window for the protection of the wiser ones. The Lord said that he suspects the plans of evil ones, and so does not approve them. But whatever the wise man decides is pleasing and acceptable to Him. The one who is greedy and wants more would bring troubles to the family, whereas the one who dislikes and avoids bribery will survive. Our God turns His ears away from the prayers of the wicked, but he hears and listens to the prayers of the virtuous people. Bright light cheers the eyes with their message of peace and love, and good news brings strength to the bones. Those who listen to the instructions being given to them end up becoming the wiser ones.

Anyone who refused discipline is his own enemy, but whoever pays heed to correction will have a full understanding of life. Wisdom and its teachings let us get accepted in the eyes of the Lord, whereas humbleness and modesty come before righteousness on the path of success.

Chapter 16
The Preparation of the Heart is Important

A man decides and makes plans for what is in his heart, but the Lord answers the prayers that are made with the mouth of a man. Humans think that they are walking the right path in their lives, but it is God who measures the intentions of one's deeds by looking into their hearts. It is, therefore, necessary to commit to the Lord, your God, in your plans for the future and let him take control of your life so that you live happily.

Because it is the Lord, our God, who takes everything in our life to its completion, even the evil ones are also destined to face hell on the Day of Judgment. God seriously despises the arrogant ones, and He will never leave them unpunished for their evil actions. God forgives our sins with love if we are faithful to Him. By being God-fearing and God-conscious in our hearts, we can possibly avoid evil in our lives. If we become successful in pleasing God with our actions, words, and our way of living, He, in return, makes our foes our friends. It is better to earn profit out of something, which is done with righteousness rather than having an advantage out of something which has been done flawlessly and without the fear of God. It is us, *humans*, who plan the course of our lives in our hearts and decide about what we will be doing next. But only God's will survives, and just His will is done, for He has the sovereign power over the universe, and He controls everything that happens in our lives. We design the course, and God creates the steps for it.

The wisdom talks about the lips of the King and states that he should never do injustice to the worthy. It states that the King always speaks the truth, so he should remain steadfast on the path of righteousness and do justice with the fear of God in his heart as the guiding light. A king can always suspect when something is going wrong in his kingdom because his throne rests on the means of honesty.

The king is always pleased by honest words, which is why he finds it nice to hear the good and wise words of the righteous ones. When the king is furious, his wrath cannot be prevented, which also brings along death. However, it is only the righteous and wise ones who can calm down His rage. When the king is pleased, His face is brightened, which depicts that there is favor, and there is life. His approval leads to His kindness, which seems like a refreshing rain in spring. It is better in this world to have knowledge than buy gold. It is even better to possess understanding rather than having the ownership of silver. Those who walk on the righteous path are successful in avoiding evil on their way because it becomes easier for them to guard their ways from wickedness as they move on. God profoundly despises the arrogant and proud ones.

Therefore, with their arrogance, they will face destruction and turmoil because an overconfident and proud soul cannot stand before God and must face a downfall. When we are with the Lord, it is better for us to grieve with the low and the suppressed ones, rather than rejoice with the arrogant people. Those who pay attention to wise instructions and teachings will lead a happy life because the one who has a firm belief in God is considered to be blessed.

Those who are wise at heart are known to be judicious because whatever they do, it becomes gracious, which encourages teaching others. Prudence or rightfulness and being careful with how you walk and talk can bring life and save the righteous ones, but foolishness brings penalties to the lost ones. Words of wisdom and righteousness are like a honeycomb, as stated by the Book of Wisdom in the Bible. They can be sweet and pleasing to the soul and have the ability to heal to the bones. Whatever appears to us as good may not be the same in the eyes of the Lord. The apparently straight pathway can lead to destruction and death at the end. The laborers and the meek ones earn through their hunger because this is what keeps them driving to work harder to survive.

Rogue is the one who makes evil plans, and their mouths are always telling lies and speaking out evil things like a blazing fire. About the perverse person, it is written in the Book of Wisdom that his conversations bring about fights, quarrels, and disputes. And when he gossips, it makes close friends go far away from each other.

A ferocious man tempts people around him and invites them to works of malevolent nature that can lead to death and eternal punishment. He who winks his eye is intending to design obstinacy. And those who purse their lips while talking are about to bring evil. Gray hair or silver hair is like a reward for a righteous man because they are considered as the crown of splendor and grace.

It is good if you turn yourself more toward patience rather than being violent like a warrior. Patience will bring humbleness and self-control, which is even better than conquering an entire city. There is a lot that can happen in this world, but the ultimate and final decision rests only with the Lord, our God.

Chapter 17
Better is A Dry Morsel with Quietness, Than A House Full of Feasting with Strife

A dry vessel is better than a house that is full of dining and food items that are prepared with discord. A wise servant has every right to rule over a disobedient son. He is also entitled to share the inheritance of the family because he has served loyally to the family. As the refining pot is for silver and the furnace is for gold, so will your Lord, the true God, test and scrutinize your heart.

Wisdom tells us that the evil person always pays heed to deceiving things, and everything that comes out of their mouth is with evil intent. The one who tells lies a lot turns his ears to the cynical and vicious tongue. Those who mock the poor and the weaker ones mock their creator instead, and those who make fun of their calamities will never be left unpunished by God. It is a moment of pride to see the children of your children in your life when you can become the pride of your children. Be the parents that your children feel proud of you.

A fool mocks the articulate speech coming out from the wiser lips, as much as lying lips to a prince. Those who take bribes for everything they do think that it will bring benefit to them in the end. But they do not know that it is only a false charm that can never come true. Those who walk by love are the ones who cover up faults and wrongdoing with their positive efforts. But those who keep repeating and mentioning the mistakes of the other person can only work as separators of close friends.

A quiet and sensible warning will have a profound impact on a sensitive and wise person. It is even better than casting a hundred whips on a fool. The evildoers are the ones who stand in rebellion against God as a result of which God will not hesitate in throwing his wrath upon them in the face of death. It is better to meet a bear who has just lost her cubs, instead of having a sit-in with a fool who is indulged in his dumb activities.

If the evil is repaid back with good then it will never leave your house. Commencing a quarrel is like breaking a dam. You give way to the tantrums to come and rest with you when you become the cause of a fight. So, it is better to drop the issue and settle it down peacefully before it gives rise to a conflict that never resolves. The one who releases the guilty and takes the innocent behind bars and punishes him is suspected by God. The Lord will not let the wrongdoer go unpunished. Why should fools and evil ones be buying wisdom for themselves when they do not understand it and never value it in their lives? A friend is always there in the times of happiness with you, whereas your brother is meant to be with you and there for you during your times of trouble and sorrow.

A senseless and a foolish person will sell out his neighbor, which implies that he follows evil people he is affiliated with and negatively affects the ones in his surroundings. Those who bring disputes out of everything are the ones who love sin, and they never find it sinful to commit an act of evil. High gates invite destruction because when you do not trust God for his provision of security, it brings only bad results.

The person with a corrupt heart will never grow, as the one whose tongue speaks evil and unreliable things will fall deeper into misery. Having a fool for a child is misery; it is no fun being the parent of a disobedient child. Being happy at heart works like medicine. Gloom and doom will just leave you sick. It is the wicked and the evil people who take bribes for every task, to distort the progression of honesty and righteousness. A wise person will always put wisdom first that has been bestowed upon him by God. Whereas the eyes of the fool are off to the edges of the earth, and they keep wandering. An evil and foolish child is a disgrace to his father and brings misery to his mother.

According to the wisdom of God, it is wrong to penalize good behavior or make good citizens pay off for the crimes that have not been committed by them. The ones with knowledge use words with limitations and always act calmly in the face of any situation. The most beneficial thing for the fools is that if they remain calm and keep silent in most matters, they might be considered as the wise ones by people around them.

Chapter 18
For By Your Words You Will Be Justified, and By Your Words You Will Be Condemned

It is stated by Wisdom present in the Book of Proverbs, Chapter 18 that a person who is unfriendly and dislikes the company of others isolates himself with selfish wants. And so, gives rise to fights against all appropriate decisions. It is the foolish people who never accept knowledge as a whole. They reject the advice and instead prefer their own thoughts and ideas. With evilness and vice, there comes disrespect and hatred as well. And then with shame, there is more criticism attached, especially by the wicked ones.

Whatever we speak through our mouths acts like a deep ocean, which may house many dangers, but when wisdom is talked out of a mouth, it works like a fountain that turns into a roaring river. It is not appropriate to be partially good with the evil ones and be unfair to the innocents. It is utter injustice in the eyes of God. One should treat them both, the virtue and the vice equally, by remaining fair to the innocent and judging the guilty based on their actions.

Since the mouth of the evil person always speaks lies; therefore, it brings them misery and conflicts, and then subsequently, they suffer from such troublesome events that they had invited themselves. These tragic events beat them down to death with misery. The evil person will keep on lashing out evil things from his mouth through his words; therefore, they are caught by their big mouths in whatever they speak. Their souls are tormented by their words.

Wisdom says that listening to gossip is just as if you are eating a delicious, sweet snack that fills your taste buds for some time. But the result of this can turn out to be bad, as it would go down to your stomach and then affect different parts of your body adversely. The one who is careless and ignorant toward his work makes a brother to that person who brings destruction to his work.

The name of the Lord is like a tower that we can rest upon and hide behind to avoid the evil in our lives. This tower is always there to protect us, and those who run toward it to get help and shelter and seek safety in his name are always successful in obtaining security from Him. On the contrary, whatever wealth the rich have, they think of it as their fort. They rely upon it so much that they believe that it is the one thing that would save them. They imagine it as a fortified city for them, where they can seek shelter when days get rough. They think that their wealth is bigger than God. But I pity them for they do not know when it would be taken away from them. When a person is on the verge of facing a downfall, he feels extremely proud of himself because he is proud of his achievements. However, honor and grace are followed by humbleness.

Those who give out their opinions before even listening to the whole topic and answer before hearing it all out are the ones who bring shame to their own names through their act of foolishness. When a soul is happy and energetic, it can conquer the enemy through positive behavior. But when it is genuinely crushed, it is gloomed in sadness. It is the sensible and intelligent people whose hearts are always seeking a handful of knowledge and information because their ears are always seeking out to hear knowledgeable things.

Your gift will make room for you and bring you before great people. The first speech given by the first person in the court is considered to be right until it is cross-questioned by someone else present there. Spin a coin to settle disputes because this keeps the bigger enemies at a distance from you.

A person can fill his stomach with the words of his mouth because those words feed him. Also, he will be satisfied with whatever he speaks. It is our tongues that become the source of life and death. Those who do good deeds and talk about virtue out of their mouths will yield the good results of their tongues in their lives and win a friend forever in the form of a good wife.

A decent wife is a blessing from God to those who have qualified to be worthy of receiving God's favor in their life. A poor person pleads for help and asks for the mercy of the rich one, whereas the rich person returns him back with cruelty. Undependable and unfaithful friends will always lead you toward destruction. However, a true friend will always be there for you, even more than a brother.

Chapter 19
Never Stop Listening

The wisdom says in the book of Proverbs in Chapter 19 that the poor ones are better, who walk in their lives without having any blame on them than the rich ones who become fools and fall prey to their own obstinacy. Having a wish without having the right knowledge is inappropriate. If you act hastily, it will definitely bring you harm. It is a man's own foolish works that lead him toward disasters in his life for which he wrongly blames God. It is true that the wealth of a rich person attracts people who want to become his friends, or somehow, they want to be affiliated with him.

However, even the closest friend leaves when a person is out of material wealth. Untrue claims and witnesses will never be let go unpunished by God, and those who lie before the court and others will be imprisoned. Most people want to win the prince's favor to acquire gifts and rewards from him. Wisdom says that when things do not go your way, everyone seems to be avoiding you, even your friends don't see you quite often, lest you may ask them for monetary help. When you do not have money, your relatives leave you alone, and even if you pursue them for help, you will find them nowhere. The one who is seeking wisdom by any means remains happy in his life because he tends to love his life. And the one who grows in knowledge will grow in peace and happiness as well. It does not suit a foolish person to live a lavish life. You may find this situation as a slave aiming to rule over the master.

The more the person is patient, the more wisdom he will get from God. If someone ignores offenses against himself, it is included to be his quality and a gift from the above. When a king is furious, his anger is like a lion's roar. His rage can become more ferocious if he is not calmed down. No one can escape the king's anger because it can be devastating and destructive as a lion's hunt.

On the other hand, his favor to a person is like dew on the grass. He also acts humbly at times and can grant approval to his people. If an offspring is foolish and evil, he can be the one in the family who would bring disgrace to his father's name. In the same way, if a wife is troublesome and creates tantrums all the time, it is like a leaking roof, which is continuously dripping water since it is not strong enough and is hollow from the inside.

A house is a blessing and is an inheritance from parents. Similarly, the wealth and property that comes down to the children is also inheritance and is counted in as a blessing too. Likewise, if a person has a wise and able wife, it is also a blessing and gift from God. Idle hands can do no good, not even for themselves, which is the reason why they remain suffering from hunger and starvation.

A lazy person is always fond of a deep sleep, and that is why he loses almost everything that is in his possession out of their lethargic behavior. There is life in the commandments of God; whoever keeps themselves close to their hearts and reminds those laws to themselves all the time are sure to have life in their houses.

When someone dislikes their ways, they can, unfortunately, lead their lives toward death without any ulterior motive. Being kind to a poor person brings God closer. God surely answers their prayers and grants the kind people the gifts of life. Also, when God is pleased by the kind act of a person of helping the poor, He also rewards them for whatever they had done. It is necessary for parents to make their children learn about discipline. They should train them to be organized in life.

This will bring them hope. Otherwise, if parents become least bothered about their children and do not make them learn about structuring their lives, it can lead their children to destruction. The person who is volatile and short-tempered will have to pay for his behavior and face punishment. Someone should be there to rescue this person and others like him. One should always hear and lend their ears to correction and advice.

They should also be prepared and ready to accept discipline and honor in their lives. In this way, they will be counted among the virtuous ones. A man decides about so many things in life. There are plenty of plans in his heart and mind. There are a lot of things that he wants to do in this world. But he should also know that only God's plan for him will bring success in his life.

A person's ultimate dream or wish is to have consistent love for themselves. However, it is superior to be poor than being a liar. If a person has a fear of the Lord in his heart, he is worthy to receive blessings in his life from God. Leading a good life keeps him away from any type of sorrows and miseries. An idle and slothful person would never strive to do anything for himself, and he would remain in distress because of his laziness. He is not even able to bring his hand to his mouth even when he is thirsty or hungry. Mockers should be punished because this teaches others valuable lessons, allowing them to understand that there is a benefit to be a simple person. It will help them to become wise by learning from the example. Similarly, the foolish and evil ones should be taught and scolded for letting them gain the knowledge of what is bad for them and, perhaps, turn their hearts around.

Children who rob their own parents and take their mother out of their house are the ones who bring dishonor and disrespect to the name of the family. Wisdom says that if you stop paying attention to teachings and instructions, you will go astray from the path of understanding and deliverance.

A witness who is dishonest will make fun of the justice, while the wicked people will take evilness and lies down their throats. Therefore, punishments have been decided already for the evil ones, for they make fun of prudence and how it operates. There will also be thrashings for people who willingly indulge in sin.

Chapter 20
Counsel in the Heart of a Person is Like Deep Water

If you drink wine, it will turn you into a perverse person. Also, if you drink beer, it will make you fall into fights and create tantrums. And this is the reason why whoever acts imprudent and behaves foolishly after having them, can never be considered as a righteous person. When the king is angry, there is a terror in his reign because he does not spare anyone in his fury. His rage is like the roar of a lion. The people who make him angry will lose their lives in the end as he ultimately controls it.

If someone avoids tantrums and fights, it will be considered as his quality and will be counted down as an honor. But unfortunately, every foolish person lures himself into a fight. The lazy ones are incredibly reluctant to do their work on time, which is the reason why they miss the plowing season, and then there is nothing left for them to harvest. A man's heart possesses numerous plans, and they are like deep waters. And the one who has the knowledge of his purpose will seek them rightly and will also be able to draw them out. Many of your friends will try to prove to you that they have unconditional love for you and that they would do anything for you, but a faithful companion is always hard to find. The ones who walk while having a fear of God in their hearts always lead blameless lives, and by doing so, their children are also blessed as a result. The king notices all evil being done in his kingdom when he sits on his throne. And then he becomes active to pick out all the wrongdoings from his nation whenever he wants.

There is no one on this earth who can claim themselves to be without sin. No one can claim their heart to be always pure and clean. Our God testifies to both the virtues and vices no matter what sources they have and whatever they do for us. Children are also known by their actions and deeds and can be judged based on their behaviors, whether or not they're pure and honest.

The Lord, our God, has created both the ears and eyes. He has created the ears to hear and listen to good things, but not foul ones. And the eyes that have been created by Him only to see what God wants us to see. Never let the sleeping habit take over you and separate you from the pleasure of sight and hearing. Do not indulge too much into sleep because you will lose all your blessings. Therefore, stay awake to witness the glory of God in your lives. If you prefer to sleep, then you will definitely lose your possessions and become poor. But if you stay awake and work diligently, you will have enough food to lead a satiated life. The buyer cries out that the item is good for nothing, but when the seller leaves, he boasts of the bargain he made.

There are gold and rubies already available in abundance, but the one who speaks the truth is the real gem of a person. As much as a jewel is rare to find, so are the ones who speak wisdom from their mouths. Hold tight to insurance on any loan to a stranger. Beware of accepting what a transient has pledged! The money earned and the food brought by unlawful means tastes good, but you never know how this lawful earning would end up in pebbles.

Plans should only be executed after obtaining proper guidance. Even if you are going to wage war, seek for instructions first. Stay far away from people who gossip all the time because this rotten conversation can betray your confidence. It is not good to curse your mother and father. Anyone who speaks ill about their parents will have to face the consequences, as their lamp will be put out during the darkness of life. Making a hurry in claiming an inheritance will not be tolerated and so not be blessed by God. Don't avenge your enemies yourself or the people who have done you wrong. Leave it all to God and let Him take your side and fight for you. If the weights are different, God will testify to them and take notice. Dishonest and deceitful means never please Him, and He will punish dishonest subjects.

No one can understand their own paths because they are determined by God Himself. An impulsive vow is a trap, and then later you will wish you could get out of it. A wise and just king is the one who would pick out evil from his empire, and He will cast the threshing wheel upon them. The spirit of a man is the lamp of the Lord searching all the inner depths of his heart.

Love and faithfulness are the two most important things that can guard the king in his castle. It is love through which the king's throne stays safe. A man's strength lies in his glory and elegance. Silver hair is the grace that he receives when he gets old. Misfortunes and injuries scrub away evil from our lives, and then punishment cleanses away the innermost existence of the spirit.

Chapter 21
God Will Examine Your Heart

The heart of the king is like a stream of water in the hands of the Lord, our benevolent God. He conduits his bounty toward all his people who make him happy by their deeds. You might think that you are walking on the right path, but it is not the case because God detests, notices, and determines your ways of life by analyzing what is in your heart. It is better to do what God wants you to do than offering a separate sacrifice to Him. You should please Him by straightening up your paths and doing what is right and acceptable in His eyes. It is much more than superficial sacrificing.

Proud heart and eyes are utterly unacceptable in the eyes of the Lord because He dislikes an unplowed field that would not yield anything but will only produce sin. Whatever a hardworking person plans bring him profit just as fast as hurry brings poverty. Making a fortune out of a mouth that speaks falsehood will pay you with smoke and lead you to spiritual death. If you make violence a part of your everyday life, then it will definitely sweep you away because you refused to act justly. The wicked man's ways will be extremely complex, but the conduct of those who behave rightly is pure and simple to follow. It is better and more comfortable to live in a corner at the roof of a house than to share a complete home with a troublesome wife. The evil ones are always in search of evil things, and they have no mercy upon their neighbors or the people in their surroundings. Those who mock will be punished, and when that time comes, pure beings will acquire knowledge.

These people will gain understanding by paying attention to what a wise man speaks to them. The wise man is careful enough that he examines the house of the evil ones closely. And then he takes the evil person to his conclusion. Those who do not listen to the cries of the poor and do not pay heed to the demands of the meek will have to pay for it in the end. Consequently, their prayers will also go unheard by God.

A secret gift that is given behind doors will always calm down anger and frustration, and it will be a joy to the righteous. In the same way, when a bribe is camouflaged, it pacifies great wrath. Justice and appropriate decisions bring happiness to wise people, but the same bring destruction to fools. If a person goes astray from the path of righteousness, then he will definitely be counted in with the evil ones; so, his life will lead to destruction and death without peace. If you love pleasure and a comforting life, you will lose it and become poor. Similarly, if you are fond of wine and olive oil, then you are never going to become rich. The evildoers become a ransom for the wiser ones, and in the same way, they show dishonest behavior for the righteous people.

It is even better to find a place to live in a desert than to live with a wife who is always fighting and manipulating the situations. Upright people save their food for the rainy days, but the evildoers gulp everything down their throats at the first chance. Those who seek righteousness and love will find happiness and growth in their lives.

The wise ones can bring down a whole city and then conquer the stronghold, in which that city's people used to have faith in because of their knowledge. People who guard their mouth and tongue—which means that they think before they speak—will be able to stay away from sorrows and miseries. An arrogant and haughty person whose name is the *"Mocker"* acts with impudent anger. A lazy man only sits and wishes for things to come to him. Therefore, his desires will lead him toward death since he did not work for those things with his own hands. A lazy man can sit all day and make wishes. But it is the righteous man who gives without sparing. Whatever a fool will sacrifice will be detested by God in all its forms because all his earnings have been acquired with evil consent and through vile means. Those who give false accounts in the court will not go unpunished and will be detested by God. Whereas, a careful listener will testify in the appropriate way.

There is no knowledge and understanding in this world. Also, there are no plans and strategies developed yet that can go against the will of the Lord, our God. Although we prepare the horses for the day of the war, only God's plan will ever work in every situation. Success only comes when we seek knowledge by following the word of our Lord.

Chapter 22
Let the Words of the Wise Be Fixed Upon Your Lips

Wisdom says that a graceful and respectful name should be desired more than having all the wealth in the world. It is better to be respected than having silver and gold. This is common for both the rich and the poor ones as the Lord, our God, is the creator of everyone. The wise person is always careful about the future.

If he senses something terrible is going to happen, he immediately takes preventive measures. He hides and takes refuge after seeing the danger. On the contrary, the fool one does not care about the future situation and keeps on moving and so faces the consequences. Humbleness is a quality that is gifted by God to those who fear Him.

When you humble yourself, you receive wealth and honor in return from God. The ways of the evil ones are not protected, and they are filled with traps and dangers. However, the ones who reserve their lives for God would protect their ways from hazards. Teach your children on the way that is determined for them by God. Make them learn how to walk straight on the path of righteousness. Once informed, they will not turn away from it even when they are old. The wealthy people tend to rule over the poor ones, whereas the debtor becomes a slave to the moneylender. If you sow injustice, then you will reap misery in return. The stick that is used for expressing anger will also be broken by God. Those who are kind to the poor and generous in their acts will be blessed by God because they share their food with the meeker ones.

When you let the mockers go out of your lives, you will also get rid of troubles and sorrows. As a result, all the fights and tantrums will also come to an end. Those who speak politely and are humble in nature speak with grace. They have the king's favor, for they will have him as their friend. God's eyes watch over wisdom. However, He gets annoyed and resented by the speeches of disloyal people.

The lazy one will never get up to fight his fears. Even if something dangerous is going to happen, he will stay inside and keep on being afraid of it without acting. He would say that there is a lion outside and that he would be killed if he went out to face it. Similarly, an illicit woman's mouth is like a deep ditch too. Those who are under the wrath of God deliberately fall into that pit. Children are prone to adopt wickedness, but the stick of discipline will keep them away from evil. Those who torment the poor and then take away their belongings will not go unpunished. Also, those who bribe the rich with gifts will come to poverty. Wisdom says that you should pay attention to what the wise people say. Wisdom speaks that you should listen to what it means.

It is pleasing to the wisdom of God when we speak it through our mouths and keep it in our hearts. It teaches us so that we have God's words embedded in our hearts, and we rest our faith in Him. Wisdom says that it has written 30 sayings for us in counsels and knowledge, to let us know the certainty of the word of truth that we may give a correction to those whom we serve.

Wisdom tells us not to take advantage of the poor and not to give false witnesses against the needy in the court. God will take up their case since He is on their side and will fight for them to bring them back to life. Wisdom forbids us to make friends with an angry person who can easily lose his cool because if we get attached to them, we will adopt their anger and wickedness too. It tells us not to be the one who enters an agreement and puts up security for loans. It tells us that if we have money to pay, then even our lodging will be taken away from under us. It tells us not to move ancient boundary markers that our forefathers had set up. This implies that we should not change the rules and regulations that were set up by our ancestors.

Wisdom asks if we had seen a skilled person in our surroundings, we should seek knowledge from them to serve the kings better. These skilled workers will never serve before the low ranked officers, as they will be reserved for the king only. Their skills will make them reach higher positions. Same can be the case with us if we are willing to learn their skills too.

Chapter 23
Restrain Yourself from Too Much Wine and Food

Wisdom says that if you are having a meal with the prince, just note what things are kept in front of you. Hold yourself back from what you are going to eat on that table. Do not become greedy for your cravings and do not have the need to have the food that is prohibited for you. Never fill yourself with overwhelming desires to acquire wealth, and never trust your own instincts that compel you to do so. The rich are like the wind. You see them one moment, and the next moment they are gone with the wind because their wealth is like a bird with wings, who will surely fly away someday.

Never eat the food out of the hands of a backstabbing person. Do not desire his choice of food because it is like someone calculating inwardly. He would tell you to eat and drink with him, but his heart is not with you, and he is thinking about all the terrible things behind your back. Never speak of wisdom in front of the foolish ones. They are the ones who do not value your wise words and will look down upon them.

Never try to displace old stones from the boundary. Do not try to move into the fences of the fatherless people, because the one who saves them is stronger, and He will do justice to them against you. Turn your heart and ears toward the teachings and direction of your elders and the wisdom of God. Never hold discipline back from a child. They will not reach the gates of death even if you spank them with a stick. In fact, do punish them with the stick to save them from death, which comes because of the lack of wisdom. They will get the message of not going to that broader path that looks pleasant but leads to ignorant death. My child, if your heart is wise, then my heart too will rejoice when your lips speak with integrity.

Do not let your heart be jealous of those who sin against God. Instead, always be excited and enthusiastic in fear of your God. You will have a great future, and your hopes will never be cut off. Hear this, my child, and try to be wise. Keep your mind on the straight path. Abstain from those who drink too much wine and eat a lot of meat, since greedy people and drunkards turn poor, literally and morally, and their laziness drags them toward rags. Hear your father from whom you got a life. Never dislike your mother, even when she is in the old age. Once you have bought the truth, do not let it go or sell it for some cheap gain. Not only the truth but also wisdom, instruction, and insight. Wise children make their parents, especially their fathers, proud of them. A man who is the father of a righteous son will have great happiness in his life. Wisdom says to make your father happy and make your mother rejoice in you.

Wisdom also says, give your heart to the Lord and let your eyes keep to His path only. As I said before, a woman who is adulterous and is evil is like a bottomless pit. A loose woman can quickly get you in trouble. She waits for you to fall into her like a bandit hiding in the corner. She is even worse than a pack of thieves because she will catch you by her evil instincts, and you get in trouble.

Who is there among you who are going through sorrow, misery, grief, and distress? Is there anyone among you who has deep bruises and has his/her eyes filled with tears of melancholy? Those of you who are in constant need of wine will fail in their lives at some point. They even thirst for a mixed wine to quench their desire. Do not look at the wine present in a cup when it is red in color. Even when it seems like it has stars in it and then its fuss sits down in the glass smoothly because, in the end, it will bite you like a snake. It will inject its venom inside you. It will make your brain work haphazardly, as you will see strange things even in the daylight. It will confuse you from recognizing even the things that you are quite familiar with. It will make you feel like a person who has gone astray, who slept the entire night at the top of high seas but had no idea about it.

You will be sleeping on top of a ship's mast, and then you will cry out that it hit you, but then you will realize that you are not hurt. You will shout, thinking that you are being beaten up, but then you will understand that you are not. You will scream and ask yourself when you will get up and get another drink.

Chapter 24
Don't envy evil men or desire to be with them, for their heart plan violence, and their words stir up trouble

Wisdom tells us not to be jealous of evil people and that we should never ask for their company because their hearts are not on the part of righteousness. Such people always try to manipulate different situations to bring out the worst results. Their lips are always discussing evil things. They mostly spend their time planning troublesome situations. Their hearts are not wise, and they are always plotting schemes against the wise ones.

Wisdom further says that a good house is built on the foundations of wisdom itself. The house that is built on the foundation of wisdom has its rooms filled with knowledge. Such a house is filled with the most beautiful concepts. The wise man will remain standing because of the great power that has been given to him by God. The people who have been gifted with the gift of knowledge and understanding should muster and cherish their blessing.

It is understood that you would need some guidance and a plan to follow to wage war. Therefore, to stand victorious in that war, you surely need the advice of knowledgeable men or counselors. Wisdom is out of fools' reach. They do not even have a clue in serious discussions. They will never get wisdom if they do not recognize its importance in their lives. Wisdom forbids the fools to open their mouths at the gate when all will be gathered.

This implies and talks about the Day of Judgment when the judgment will be in process for each one of us in complete detail. The people who plan evil schemes against others will be regarded as the schemers or the plotters. The person who is always cooking up evil plans is a disgrace to mankind. The evil plans that are created by the schemer will be included in the category of sin.

A mocker will be despised by the people. If a person becomes weak in the time of trouble and amid sorrows, he will be considered as a person with no strengths. This will make him a weak person because he failed to face the difficulties in his life. Wisdom says that we should help and save those who are in trouble and are near death. We must hold the hands of those who are nearly slaughtered by the miseries in their lives. Those who want to end their lives because of the adversities should be saved and brought back to life. Wisdom says that if you say that it was nothing that you knew about, then you are on the wrong path. Because He who weighs your heart knows it, and He who protects you has the idea of everything you do. Wisdom then asks that if we have such an ignorant behavior toward the oppressed, would not God, who sits above all, judge us? He will because He knows how to repay each one of us according to our deeds.

Wisdom says, *"My son, have some honey and eat it because it is good for you. It is sweet straight out from the honeycomb, and you will find it delicious."* The honeycomb is the knowledge of wisdom, which is the food for our souls. Wisdom is the honey that is given to us by God. If you are successful in finding and getting that honey, you should know that it is for your own good. Once you have acquired that honey, try not to lose it ever. Because the honey of wisdom will bring hope for you in your life. This hope is eternal and will never leave you. Never keep waiting near the house of the righteous men, because it is something that the thieves do.

Do not be like the thieves who sit in the dark and wait for the wise man to come out of his house so that they rob him. Do not try to plunder their homes. Do not steal from the wise ones, neither rob them of their money. It will be of no use to you because God is with them and will save them. A wise man will fall seven times but will soon get up because God will not let him lie down on the ground for long.

The wicked, on the other hand, will stumble and fall at the precise time when sorrows and miseries hit them. Do not be glad and happy when your enemy falls down. Never rejoice at their demise or downfall. Do not mock their deterioration. Because if you do so, God is watching you. So do not let Him turn his wrath away from the evils and bring it upon you. Fear the Lord for

His ways are unusual and different. Do not try to be upset because of the evil people and their wrongdoings. Never be jealous of their endeavors because the evil ones have no secure future. The coming days of the evil ones are not bright because their lamp will soon be extinguished. Wisdom says, *"Fear the Lord, my son. For He is the King of heaven and earth. Never form links with the league of the rebels. Because you never know when destruction will fall upon them."* Also, we don't know when God is going to bring His wrath upon them. It is not right to show partiality in judgment. Your decisions should never be biased. If you side with the guilty and declare them innocent, you will be cursed by people and condemned by countries. However, it will go well with those who convict the guilty, as a generous blessing will come to them. An honest reply is as gentle as a kiss.

Wisdom guides us to arrange our exterior works in order. It tells us to keep our fields prepared and then proceed to build our house. It tells us never to bear witness against our neighbors that count the people around us. Your witness should never be without the evidence. Will you use your lips for those false pieces of evidence?

Never try to take revenge on your own. For it is not your job to do. Leave it on God, the Father, and He will avenge you. Wisdom says that it visited the field of a lazy person. His field is past the vineyard. This lazy person seemed to have no sense at all because the condition of his field is inappropriate. There were thorns that had grown out everywhere. Weed had covered the ground while the stones were full of ruins. Behold! There were nettles covering its face, and its stone wall was broken down. Wisdom says that it realized the situation of the field and learned a lesson from that. The learning was that even a short nap or the slightest rest could cause destruction. The folding of the hands indicates that the person owning the fields is not concerned about his farm and is quite reluctant in applying his full efforts. Therefore, poverty will come to them like a thief, while paucity will cover them from every side like an armed soldier.

Chapter 25
Wise sayings of Solomon

The wise sayings of Solomon continue in this chapter of the Book of Proverbs as well. These wise sayings have been compiled by the wise man, Hezekiah, King of Judah. Wisdom says that God finds happiness in concealing matters. By this, it indicates that God covers up the flaws of a wise person and hides them from the rest of the world.

He is always there to keep our secrets and conceals them, and then never recalls them for the world to see them. He also conceals things that are meant to be hidden from the anxious mind of mankind. There are certain matters that are kept hidden by God Himself. However, it is the scientists and scholars in the world who like to discover them, violating the boundaries that have been kept around those secrets.

As heaven is high and the earth is deep, so are the hearts of the rich men that can never be investigated. Get rid of the impurities from the silver. The silversmith will create a precious vessel out of that pure form of silver. The wicked should be removed from the presence of the King, who is

Just. This will lead the way in establishing the King's throne as the throne of righteousness. Do not try to elevate yourself in the presence of the King. Never try to adjust yourself among the great men in the King's court. It will be honorable for you if the King himself asks you to come and sit with him at a higher place. It will be better for you if the King regards you among the nobles rather than he insults you to leave the place where the great men are seated.

Regardless of the type of matter you are an eyewitness of, do not rush to bring it to the court. Because if that turns out to be false evidence and your neighbor calls you an untrue witness, what will you do to save face? It will consequently bring shame to you. If you bring your neighbor to the court, do not try to let down the trust of others. Otherwise, the person who knows that you are giving a false witness will charge you with a penalty, which will consequently bring shame to your name.

A word spoken at the right time is like golden apples placed on a tray of silver. It is like a wise decision made by a wise man. The wise choice is like a fine gold earring or a gold ornament, reproofing a wise judge to lend an ear. Those who send their boss a trustworthy messenger, are like the coolness of snow on a harvest day. He refreshes the life of his master. The one who boasts about gifts that have never been given to him by God is like the empty clouds without the rain. A soft-spoken person with gentle words can melt a stone and can also break a bone. While with the help of patience, a strict ruler can be convinced. Wisdom says that if you find honey (of wisdom, as explained in the previous chapter), eat it. But, eat it in an adequate amount, so that you do not throw it out of your mouth. Do not go to your neighbor's house that often, because it will make you lose your worth in the eyes of your neighbor.

The person who gives a false witness against a neighbor (a neighbor indicates the people in your surroundings) is like a sharp knife, a sword, or an arrow. If a wise man is in trouble and he trusts an unwise man, it is like trusting a broken tooth or a lame foot. The one who sings songs to a person who is sad and has a heavy heart filled with sorrows is like the one who takes off the clothes of another person in winter. Or like the one who puts salt on the open wounds of an injured person. Wisdom says that if your enemy is starving and is dying of hunger, it is good that you feed him. If he is thirsty, you should give him something to drink so that his thirst is quenched. Because when you do this to your enemy, feeding him and quenching his thirst, you will do an act of kindness. This kindness will be equal to putting burning coals on his head. The Lord will then reward you for this act of humbleness against your enemy. The tongue that speaks evil about others and backbites is like the wind that flies from the north and brings unexpected rain.

Wisdom says that it is better to live at a corner on the roof than to live with evil and foolish wife in a spacious house. The good news that arrives from a land that is far away is so soothing. It is like an exhausted man getting cold water in weariness. If a righteous man falls down in front of a wicked person, it is like falling down into a puddle of mud. It is not good for you to eat extra honey after it has already filled your belly.

Wisdom beyond your knowledge can be harmful to you, for it is not allowed by God. It is not regarded as honorable to look for the truths that are beyond our understanding. Wisdom, at the end of this chapter, says that a person who cannot have self-control in his life is like a city where the walls are broken, and the defender is unable to protect itself from the enemy's invasion.

Chapter 26
Don't Respond To the Stupidity of a Fool

Wisdom says that honor does not suit a fool just like snow does not suit in summer or rain at the time of harvest. Like the sparrow in its wandering, and like the swallow in its flying, the causeless curse doesn't alight. If the fools do not pay attention to the wise instructions, there should be a knife on their backs to teach them a lesson, just like there is a whip for the horses and a bridle for the donkeys. If a foolish person asks you a question out of foolishness, do not answer him, because there are chances that you might become just like them.

Answer them according to their mentality so that they do not consider themselves as a wise person. If you want to convey a message to someone, but you are sending it by the hands of a foolish person, it is like drinking poison or committing suicide. The proverbs of wisdom in the mouth of an unwise person are like the unmoving and lifeless legs of a lame man. If you give an evil and foolish man honor that he is not worthy of, it is like placing a stone in a sling. If proverbs from the book of wisdom are heard from the mouth of a fool, it is like a thorn bush in the hands of a drunkard. Wisdom says that if a wise person hires a foolish or an evil person for a job, it is like hiring a person who throws stones on the passersby and gets them injured for no reason. Fools who return to their evildoings are like a dog who licks his own vomit. Have you noticed someone who considers himself as a wise person? He would not be approved in the eyes of God.

It is even worse to look for hope in a fool. Wisdom says that a lazy man shouts that there is a lion at the door and on the street. Therefore, he fears and stays inside the house and never gets up from his bed. As a door turns on its hinges, so is a lazy man who turns sides on his own bed but does not get up and go to work. A lethargic man puts his hand in the dish, but he is too lazy to bring it to his own mouth.

Such a person thinks he is wise and considers himself as a knowledgeable person. He thinks he is wiser than those seven men who bring evidence to the court. A person who interferes in a fight of a stranger is like the one who grabs a dog by his ear. It does not suit for a wise man to have his say in a stranger's matter. Like a madman who throws flaming darts and deadly arrows, so is the person who deceives his neighbor and says that he was only joking. Wisdom says that a quarrel always comes to an end if there is no gossip involved. When foolish conversations are included in a discussion, it gives rise to an argument. It is just like a fire does not burn without a flame. An argumentative person in a dispute is like kerosene thrown on a fire.

The words from a conversation, which is about backbiting and gossip, are like delicious bites that cannot be resisted. These bites are so scrumptious that they get easily digested. False talks from an evil heart are for the disbelievers. Those evil talks are like silver coated stones that are not real from the inside. Wisdom says that a person whose heart is not pure toward others always holds grudges against others and then hides them.

He lies all the time that he cares about other people, while in reality, he does not. Whenever a deceitful person speaks softly and delivers to you those honey and sugarcoated praises, never believe him, for his heart is full of hatred and betrayal. Even if he tries to hide his treachery and dishonor against the wise men, still his hatred and follies will be unveiled in front of everyone in the court. The Wisdom of

Solomon says that whoever digs a pit for the wise man to fall in it, will fall into that pit hole himself. And whoever rolls over a stone against the prudent, will himself be affected by it. It calls out evil people and warns them to make plans against the people of God.

For they will themselves be hit by those calamities that they had been scheming against the shrewd ones. Therefore, God is with the righteous men and will protect them against all evil. In the end, the Wisdom of King Solomon says that the tongue of the evil despises the people it has hurt before. Also, a flattering mouth is always on the verge of spreading rumors that bring disasters.

Chapter 27
Never Boast About Tomorrow

Wisdom says never boast about tomorrow because you never know what is going to happen the next day. Do not self-praise your achievements. Let other people praise your work only. It is better if your accomplishments are appreciated by others rather than yourself. Consequently, self-boasting is a sin in the eyes of God. Never be provoked by a fool.

Never take his advice in life, for they are more substantial than the burden of stone and sand. Remember, jealousy is worse than anger and fury. An angry man would show his anger openly, and a furious man's fury is always obvious, but jealousy stays inside a man's heart and burns him like a silent fire.

Wisdom says that it is important to rebuke and scold a person who acts foolishly openly, rather than showing him hidden love, which can be a malicious act. A friend who hurts sometimes can be trusted, but an enemy's kiss should always be recognized, for they are always manipulating. A person who is already full does not need a honeycomb to satisfy himself. But for a person who is starving already, even a bite from a bitter thing just to get rid of his hunger is justified. He would forget the bitterness, and it would taste sweet for him. Wisdom says that a person who runs away from his house is like a bird who wanders away from its nest and gets lost in the air. Just like the fragrance and essence of a perfume that brings happiness to the heart, so is the soothing and heartily advice of a faithful friend.

Do not leave the friend who is loyal to you, or don't even leave your friend who is faithful to your father. Whenever you are in trouble, do not ask for help from your brother, because wisdom says that it is better to ask for help from a faithful friend who lives nearer to your house, rather than disturbing your brother who lives far away.

My son, the wisdom says, be nice to me and hear what I mean, for this will give me the strength to answer those who question me. Wisdom says that a sage would always foresee the danger, and they would make arrangements for finding shelter in a safer place before a calamity. Meanwhile, the foolish ones move forward even after seeing the danger ahead and then face the consequences by paying the price of such dumb acts.

You are allowed to take away the clothes of the one who sides with a stranger. You can also hold back anything from a person who witnesses in favor of an unknown man. Wisdom says that if someone prays for their neighbor and blesses them early in the morning, they're most likely to suffer the curse. It says that an evil wife is like the continuous dripping of water from a broken roof in the days of the rainy season.

If anyone tries to stop that evil wife from fighting without reason, then they are trying in vain because it is useless to restrain her. It is just like trying to hold oil with your hand. Just as iron is sharpened with another piece of iron, so is a man known by the company he keeps. Wisdom says that a person who guards around the tree of fig all the time will be blessed abundantly.

Also, the person who tries to protect the owner of that fig tree will get rewards and blessings from God. Just as you can see your own face in the water, so are the acts of a man visible to the world. Moreover, the life of a person reflects the nature of his heart. Just as the abyss is never satisfied by the number of souls it swallows, and just how the pit of destruction remains discontented, the eyes of humans are never satisfied with what they want to see. The purity of silver and gold is always tested by putting them in the fire. In the same way, the purity of a man's heart is checked by giving him a little fame or problem. Wisdom says that even if you grind a fool with a mortar, and that if you keep grinding them along with the grains, you can never take their foolishness and evilness away from them.

These two traits, foolishness and evilness, stick with them forever and can never be separated from them. Wisdom advises us to take care of our flock of sheep. It is, therefore, compulsory for us to thoroughly look after our belongings. It is of dire importance that they should be protected, and attention should be given to them.

You need to take good care of the things that belong to you or the ones that you have earned; because riches do not stay with you forever, and also fame and popularity can never be your friend for the rest of your life. They will go away one day if you do not take care of them or pay attention to them. When the hay is cleared from the field, you can see the greenery. Then the food for your cattle is collected by cutting away that greenery, which includes bushes and leaves.

And when your sheep eat the best food provided to them, they produce excellent quality of wool to make the sweaters that would cover you up in winters. Also, your cattle will be able to produce good quality of milk, which can be enough to feed your family and help the neighbors too. This milk will also be enough to feed your servants.

Chapter 28
A Person of Understanding and Knowledge Right Will Be Prolonged

Wisdom says that even if the wicked are not being pursued, they still keep running. But the prudent ones are wise enough to face any difficulty as boldly as a lion. The wicked are aware of their mistakes and sins, which is why they are always under the guilt that they would get caught, and so they keep running.

Even if the country is in a state of transgression and misdemeanor, it will still be governed by wise men and other people having just knowledge and understanding. A poor man who does evil to another poor person is definitely like the rain that sweeps away everything, including food and goods as well when it pours heavily on the land.

Wisdom says that those who reject the teachings of prudence and the law that has been given by God, take side with the wicked people, and favor them in their evil actions. On the contrary, the people who spend their lives in fear of the Lord by acting upon his given laws, live their lives in satisfaction and contentment. Foolish men are not aware of the wise teachings from the Word of God; they do not even know judgment. But those who are wise tend to have the knowledge and understanding of all the things that God wants them to do. The ways adopted by the poor people are better because they stand blameless in the eyes of God, as compared to the ones who have all the riches in the world and are included in the category of the perverse.

The son of a prudent man will always try to pay attention to the wise instructions of his father. Whereas, the son of a man whose eyes see lust and greed in the world would definitely bring shame to the name of his father. A person who gathers his wealth through unlawful means, whose ways are not wise in the eyes of the Lord, and who does not have mercy for the poor in his heart, is actually collecting his wealth for the person who is humble and polite to the poor.

Wisdom says that if the people on earth turn a deaf ear to its instructions and do not pay attention to what it advises, then they are responsible themselves for their own destruction as even their prayers are not acceptable to the Lord. Whoever digs a pit hole for a wise person and misguides him on the wrong path that he is not aware of, will fall into his own prepared hole. It also implies that if the wicked misguides a wise one, then they will have to face the consequences for themselves on their own as the Lord will avenge them for doing wrong to the wise ones. However, the people who remain blameless are the most likely to receive the blessings from above.

The rich people are blinded by their own wealth. They think they can do anything in this world on the basis of their riches. They think they are wise enough to even become wise in front of the Lord just because they are wealthy enough. They believe that if they spend their money on the poor and do other philanthropic works, it will be acceptable in the eyes of the Lord even without remembering to praise His holy name.

Well, wisdom says that it is a shame for them because the ones who are weaker, meek, and even poor but are wise in the eyes of the Lord can see that all of their riches, fame, and power cannot save them from the wrath of God. When the righteous man is elevated on the upper level by God, the world rejoices with him. They feel happy about his success because they know that he will fulfill his tasks wisely.

However, when an evil person gets fame and power, people around him get worried and become afraid of his rise because they know that his ways are evil, and he will never be humble and merciful to them. Wisdom says that the people who hide their sins and conceal them behind thick walls will never be successful in moving on in their lives. Those who never confess to their sins think that God cannot see; therefore, they will find it difficult to overcome their shortcomings and bad habits.

However, those who confess and repent from their sins are the most likely to receive blessings of happiness from the Lord. The Lord blesses them and forgives them of their sins. People who spend their lives in fear of the Lord are blessed by Him. But those who make their hearts stiff and do not pay attention to the instructions given to us by the word of God, are earning miseries and troubles for themselves.

A wicked tyrant and an evil dictator are like a lion who keeps on roaring and is in need to hunt for his victims all the time. He is also like a grizzly bear who looks for his hunt and is ready to eat them alive. A tyrant's reign will be called as the reign of terror. He finds happiness in practicing evil ways to harm people. But the one ruler who hates wickedness and treachery will be blessed with a long-lasting and peaceful reign. The person who is guilty of murder will himself run toward getting buried in the grave, and no one should ever stop him because this would be his fate. The wage of sin is death. The person whose walk is pure with God will get all the goods in his life.

But the person who walks on the twisted path will one day fall into a pit of darkness. Wisdom says that people who work wholeheartedly on their fields and farms will get the fruit of their hard work one day and will be blessed with the fruits of joy and abundance. Whereas, the people who believe in fantasies and think that things will fall from heaven for them, and they will have to do nothing, will suffer from poverty throughout their lives.

A person who is faithful to God and walks righteously on the path of wisdom will be blessed with riches and power. But the one who is curious about getting rich in a short span of time and through evil means will never be let go without receiving due punishment. Partiality can also be a sin in the eyes of God. Taking sides with evil ways just to earn your bread is not considered wise before God. But still, an evil man would try out his evil and selfish ways to feed himself.

The people who are anxious about acquiring wealth and cannot wait for the good times to come are unaware of the fact that there is darkness at the end of the road of evil ways for them. They will definitely have to go through poverty in their near futures. If a person sees something evil being done and then tries to stop it, he will be rewarded by the Lord. While, on the other hand, the person who flatters with a false mouth and does not resist the evil ways will be punished in the end.

Wisdom says that whoever steals from their parents and then tries to justify their evil deeds in front of them will suffer from the wrath of God. They are the ones who are on the side of the monster of destruction. It is the greedy person whose greed for tantrums can never be contended. He will always try out ways to give rise to quarrels and disputes.

Whereas, the people who have their firm belief in God, our Lord, will have prosperous futures. Those who believe in themselves are the ones who are counted among the foolish ones. They are stupid enough to have faith in themselves, but the people who spend their lives according to the wisdom of God will always be safe in His grace. The hands of the wise people who are always ready to give out to the needy will never suffer from poverty, and their houses will always be abundantly blessed. But those who do not stretch their hands out, for the process of giving, will inevitably suffer from curses. People who close their eyes from the realities in their surroundings will go through calamities.

Wisdom, at the end of this chapter, says that when an evil person is made a ruler of a country, he becomes a tyrant who torments his people, and during his reign, his nation suffers because of him. But at the same time, when that evil person goes through troubles, it gives rise to the weak and the wiser people to power.

Chapter 29
Don't be blind to the wisdom of God

Wisdom says that people who refuse to bow down and accept their mistakes are the most likely to get destroyed without having anyone to save them. At times when the wise people are blessed with a chance to rise and have power, they find that people rejoice in their success. But when an evil person gains authority, people dislike his rule.

A man who lives according to the teachings of wisdom and applies them to his everyday activities is loved by his father because he is the one who brings joy and grace to the family. But the one who is friends with the unethical people, like prostitutes, and likes to spend time in their company, spends his wealth on evil doings.

If justice prevails in a country with the wise efforts of a just ruler, then the country thrives, gains prosperity, and becomes stable enough to fight all kinds of situations, whereas the rulers who receive a bribe and are greedy for money bring melancholy and disgrace to the nation by tearing it down. A man who flatters his neighbor weaves a net or a trap for him to fall in it. However, evil people fall into their mistakes and become victims of their own evil schemes. Whereas, the righteous men rejoice and sing the praises of the Lord when they are blessed with the fruits of happiness. The wise men and the righteous people are more concerned about bringing justice to the poor, needy, and deserving people. While the evil and the wicked ones have no such concerns for the meeker ones because of their selfish attitudes.

Wisdom says that people who make fun of the wise ones cause many disputes in the city. However, righteous people help anger, and conflicts go away with their virtuous vibes. If a righteous person takes the help of a foolish person in the matters of the court to get his dispute solved and be justified, then he is in great danger, because a foolish person can never provide useful advice to a wise person.

Never expect any good coming out from an evil source. There is no peace guaranteed at the hands of an evil man. Malevolent men who are always thirsty for someone's blood are always looking and searching for reasons to kill. Whenever they get a chance, they murder the righteous people because they are the ones who rebuke them from sinning against God. Evil and foolish people give way to their foolish attitude and never stop themselves from being angry or unwise. Whereas, the ones who tend to calm themselves down and avoid social conflicts are worthy to receive the blessings of God. When a ruler of a country listens to false statements and is ready to justify them in front of the court, then all of his officials will also adopt the evil and false ways of governing a country. When the base of a building is built on the foundation of lies and deceit, then the entire building will be known as an epitome of lies.

The one thing that is common in both the poor and the oppressed is that their prayers are heard by God, and He grants them wisdom, which becomes the sight to their eyes. When a king is true to his nation and adopts the wise conducts to govern, then his kingdom will grow beyond the limits, and his throne will be established forever by the Lord.

It is better to rebuke a boy when he makes a mistake even at an early age. It is better to teach him with the help of a stick, as that would teach him respect, and he will never try to bring disgrace to the name of his parents. There are times when even wicked people thrive and reach a better position in their lives. But when that time comes, sins follow them, and they cannot get away with it for long. The wicked people indulge themselves in evildoings by having faith in their wealth, but they do not know that the wrath of God awaits them in the end. When they suffer, the righteous will be there to witness their downfall. Wisdom says to teach your children the rules and regulations of discipline. It makes their lives more organized so that in the end, they bring peace and happiness to the family.

Where there is no revelation, and the people are left without the visions from God, it is easier for the people to cast off their restraints. Instructions from God are necessary to live a peaceful life, and where there are no instructions, especially from above, people are unleashed, and they can easily get free from their shackles.

A servant will never learn from words only, for they will continue doing what they are prohibited from doing. They might understand you, but they will never obey you. Have you noticed a person who speaks fast without any reason or purpose? God knows them and identifies them, for they show that a fool has more hope to be saved than them. A person who even raises his servant with that care and attention as given to his real son, will one day end up with that servant becoming his son. Wisdom says that an angry person is always ready to bring up tantrums and conflicts in his surroundings. And a person who is hot-tempered and gets furious easily is more prone to committing sin than others who normally react to situations. Arrogant people are more likely to go through troubles and miserable situations, but those who are humble at heart and polite in their behavior will acquire honor and grace.

Those who accompany thieves and help them in robberies and criminal activities are their own enemies because they are doing wrong with their own selves, by putting themselves in dangerous situations while already being aware of the consequences. Sometimes these people, who act as helpers to the criminals, are forced to take an oath and promise not to open their mouths against them.

If you are afraid that some people around you will bring misery upon you, then refrain from being near them. But those who have their firm beliefs in the Lord will save themselves from falling into that hole of darkness. Most of the people seek the favor of the ruler and want the decision to be made in their favor. However, they should know that every decision that is taken on earth is made by the will of

God. Therefore, they should obey the word of God. Wise people can judge and testify against the dishonest and unwise people when they are required. This implies that a wise man despises the evil ones, while the unjust and unwise people hate the company of the righteous men.

Chapter 30
We need Yahweh

This chapter of the book of Proverbs includes the wise sayings of Agur, son of Jakeh. This man spoke to Ithiel in the following words. He said to God that he was tired in his strength, but he could still be victorious. He said that he was only a brutal man or a warrior who was there to fight in wars. Therefore, he did not have an understanding of human knowledge.

He does not know about the wisdom of God, nor does he have any knowledge about the Lord. He has never known about the existence of God, as he is unaware of the fact that only He is the creator of the universe. He is the one who has ascended to heavens and will descend to earth one day. He does not know that God is the one who has held up the shutters of the wind that make the sky.

He is unaware of the fact that God, the Lord, is the one who has gathered the water on earth in a cloak, and He, who has created the ends of the earth and demarcated the boundaries. He asks about the Lord's name, as he does not know. Neither does he know the name of His only son. He asks the ones who know. He says that each and every word that comes out of the mouth of the Lord is without any mistake and flawless. God becomes the shield to the people who take shelter under His mighty wings. Never try to modify or make additions to whatever God says, because the results of this can be troublesome for you. God will rebuke you for the alterations in His commandments or sayings, and He will also declare you as a liar.

Agur asks God about two things. Firstly, he asks God not to refuse him before his death. Secondly, he asks God to keep lies and vanity away from him. He also asks God only to grant him enough that he is not left behind as a poor man, but not grant him too much that would make him an arrogant person. He asks God only to bless him with his daily bread. Everything that he needs for a day.

He is afraid of the state where he receives so much from the Lord, and then (God forbids) denies His existence and forgets Him. He says that do not insult a servant, or else they would instead stand up and curse you. You never know when God would hear their prayers against you, and you will have to pay for it. There are also some people in this world who tend to curse their fathers and never try to bless their mothers. They are always saying bad things about their parents, and so despise them. There are also those people in this world who think that they are entirely pure and have been cleaned already. They feel that their actions and deeds are pure and cleansed, both in the eyes of man and God as well. But at the same time, they are unaware of the truth that their righteousness is like the ashes from something that has been burnt.

It is useless in front of God when they do all the good in the world without knowing and praising the true God. They do not know that their existence is still covered in filth and dirt. People who are arrogant enough to look down upon others will not go unpunished. Those who look with a sharp eye and in an insulting manner will have to pay for their acts.

People who have their teeth as sharp as swords are ever ready to cut out the resources of the wise ones with the words out of their mouths. Those who have their jaws as severe as knives are ready to bite the good out of the lives of the prudent ones. Such people are there to demolish the poor from the face of the earth. And also, they are ready to allow the needy ones to vanish from the face of mankind. Greed has been identified here in this chapter with a leech that has two daughters. It implies that greedy people know only two things. They are always crying out, *"give me, give me."* There are also other three things that remain uncontended. In fact, there are four that refuse to say the word 'enough.' Those who mock their fathers and look down upon their mothers will suffer the wrath of God because their eyes will be plucked out by the ravens of the valley and will be eaten off by the vultures.

He (Agur) says that there are four things that amaze him. The first is the way of an eagle flying in the sky; the second is how a snake crawls on the rocks; the third is, how a ship sails in the high seas. And fourth, how a man acts with a young woman. He explains the ways of an adulterous woman.

She eats out of the entire thing and then wipes her mouth, which means that she performs the sinful acts and cleans the place. Yet, she still tries to come clean and justifies that she has done nothing wrong. There are three things that the earth and the entire humanity is shaken from. In fact, there are four that people can hardly stand up to. Firstly, when a servant becomes a leader or a ruler. Secondly, a fool who does not know God and still gets plenty to eat. Thirdly, a disgraceful woman who gets married. And fourthly, a servant who takes the place of her mistress. There are four things on this earth that are small but can be regarded as the wisest on earth. Look at those ants. They are among the smallest creatures on earth, yet they struggle a lot to collect food in the summers. Look at the Hyraxes that are the creatures with the lowest strength, but still, they strive to build their places to live in the crags.

Then there are locusts that have no king, but still, they move forward in ranks. There is a lizard that is easy to catch with a hand, but still, it is the one creature that is also found in the kings' palaces. There are three things that act important when they walk. There are, in fact, four that can move the foundations of a state.

Firstly, the lion is the most powerful creature among all the beasts. He is the warrior among the animal and runs away from nothing. Secondly, there is this rooster that walks proudly. Thirdly, a He-goat. And lastly, a king getting insecure about the rebellion. If you have been foolish enough to become proud and make plans against other people, stop and think about what you are doing. Just as butter is produced by churning cream and blood comes out of the nose when it is twisted, so does conflict arise, as a result of anger.

Chapter 31
The words of King Lemuel's Mother

This chapter from the book of proverbs includes the wise sayings of the mother of King Lemuel. This chapter discusses everything that she taught his son. She calls her son the answer to her prayers. She advises her son not to spend his strength and youth on women because they can become the cause of him being ruined. These women destroy kings, so do not waste yourself on them. It does not suit a king to drink wine.

Whilst it does not even seem appropriate for rulers to have a desire for beer because it can result in kings and rulers, forgetting about the commandments of the Lord. And also, they might remember nothing about what has been decreed by Him. They might also oppress the weaker ones from their rights and forget that it has been forbidden by the Lord. Beer is for those who are about to die and end up with miserable lives. Give wine to the ones who are cruel and wicked. Give them beer to drink, and they will forget their poverty and weakness.

They will get drunk and forget about all their sorrows and troubles. You need to speak the words out of your mouth in favor of the ones who are deprived of their own rights. Say something for them and help the ones who are impoverished. Talk out for those who are helpless. Defend them and help them out in their time of troubles. Help them out in the coming hour of their miseries.

Make the right judgment and decide fairly for them, so that they are dealt with justice. In this chapter, the character of a noble wife has also been discussed. It is hard to find the wife of a noble character. The one who is clean and pure because their worth is more than the precious gems and stones. The husband of a virtuous wife has complete confidence in her. He trusts her with all of his heart because she has nothing in her personality that is worth thinking otherwise.

A noble wife is always there for her husband to bring him all the good things instead of the bad ones. She would always protect her husband and be by his side to support him for the rest of her life. She looks for wool and flax and gathers them. She works around her house with anxious hands. A noble wife is like the ship of a trader. She gathers her food from far out places for the rainy days, so that nothing in her house gets scarce. She wakes up in the middle of the night and feeds her family if they are hungry. She also gives shares to her female servants and helps them out in their need. She analyzes the field, and if she thinks it is suitable for her, she decides to purchase it. She then owns a piece of land that belongs to her. The next thing she does is to earn from that piece of land by planting a vineyard. She gets herself prepared for work with strong ambitions. She sets her goals in front of herself and then walks vigorously toward them. She has strong arms and works with passion. She notices that her business is doing her good.

Her lamp never goes out at night, and there is always light in her house, even in the dark. She makes her own thread and weaves her own clothes. She always gives to the poor and helps those who need it. At the time of winters, she is not afraid of the cold winds. She has already prepared for the snow. Her family has warm clothes to wear in winter and protect themselves from the cold winds. She creates her bed coverings with a fine piece of cloth. Her own dresses are sewed from fine linen. The husband of a noble wife is respected across the country.

When he sits among the elders, his conversation is worth praising. This is all because his wife supports him. She sews garments made out of linen, which is of amazing quality. She creates clothes and then sells them in the market. She provides sashes to the traders as well. She is filled with strength and passion. Other people feel honored to be around her. She is not afraid of the days that are yet to come, and thus, she smiles because she is already prepared. A noble wife always speaks wisdom and truth. She never lies and does justice with everyone. She is always there to advise good instructions because she is wise with her own self as well. She is a prudent wife who knows humbleness and mercy. A noble wife always takes care of her domestic chores. She never sits free and keeps on working at her house. She does not eat the bread of idleness because she thinks that it is unlawful for her.

She is praised by her husband, and her children call her a blessed woman. Her husband praises her for her nobility and tells her that she has earned dignity over all the other women who cannot be as wise as her. Beauty is deceiving, and splendor does not last for long; it is unsustainable. However, a noble wife with a wise character is not only to be praised by her husband and other people around her, but also by the Lord himself. Give her what she deserves! Praise her for all of her works that she has done with her own hands. Let her achievements be praised around the world so that she earns the recognition that she deserves.